How we came to
MISUNDERSTAND EVERYTHING

Mike Smart

June 2021

Dedicated to Margaret

Acknowledgements

I am grateful to many people for their thoughtful commentary on earlier versions and helpful suggestions about the process of publishing a book: Paul Paterson, Clifford Winston, Nicki Hutley, Imelda Brewster, Tony Butler, Alan Close, Euan Morton, Andrew Stone, Bates Gill, Hugo Harmstorf, Liz Livingstone, Neroli McSherry, Bruce Hurwit, Peter Brady, Ed Willett, Ron Ben-David, Neil Douglas as well as my family Florence, Hugo and Edward Smart and Margaret Kay. I would also like to thank Gabrielle Tydd for designing the cover and typesetting the book.

CONTENTS

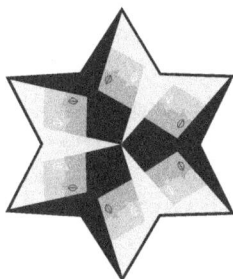

1
OVERVIEW

The Trump experience has led us to question our understanding of the world. Everyone seems to agree that we're not getting what we wanted. No one seems to agree on how to design a supervisory structure that will give it to us. Slightly more than half the people take the view that a rule of law, based on facts and logic, with rules determined by a majority of citizens would be best. I don't understand why this group is so perilously close to being a minority.

I'm not sure what to say about the significant number of people who take a different view. Their prevalence, their loudness and their absolute insistence is a mystery to me. That is another way that the Trump experience has led me to question my understanding.

Of course, Trump encouraged his followers to question their understanding of epidemiology, justice for all, friend and foe, and even something as basic as counting votes. His motives seem transparent enough, so I am not going to explore them here. My topic is the rise of misunderstanding itself.

It is popular to diagnose Trump as more of a symptom than a cause of our predicament. Democracy and science were under attack even before he decided to play politics with them. The first third of this book explains those developments.

I do not personally subscribe to the view that Trump is a mere passenger on this historic voyage to chaos. There is no denying his captaincy or his culpability for our current trajectory. A different president, even a staunch conservative, would have been less reckless and our outcomes would have been better.

In the middle third of this book, I present some blog posts I wrote as the pandemic took hold in 2020 and then as the insurrection at the Capitol played out in 2021. My purpose then and now is to consider what these shocking events tell us about ourselves, what might return to normal once everyone calms down, and what will change irrevocably.

The final third of this book contemplates some hypothetical futures and what hope we can derive from humankind's ingenuity. There is some very encouraging stuff there. After all, we're talking about a species with an opposable thumb.

The bread in this sandwich is excerpted from an earlier book of mine entitled "Economics even a President could understand." Clearly I misjudged that.

The question on everyone's mind: is there hope? Will things turn out all right in the end? I approach this from a hopeful point of view. I am optimistic that human compassion and ingenuity will win out in the longer run. But I am not so foolish as to believe that good guys always win or that the path to utopia is guaranteed by good intentions alone. To personalise the impersonal, chaos is a determined adversary. Let us together think up some better strategies to keep it at bay.

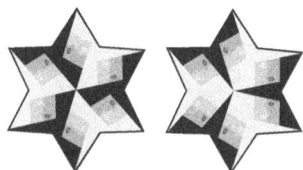

PART 1

MISUNDERSTANDING THE PAST

2
WHERE DID IT ALL GO WRONG?

I don't feel comfortable with the way the world is going, and I'm guessing you don't either. Despite all our cleverness, we seem to be making some regrettable choices on the climate, on weapons, on equality and even on some apparently simple tasks like keeping the drinking water safe and the electricity supply working. The puzzling question is why an intelligent race of beings keeps making bad choices on the things that matter the most?

In this chapter I will touch on three themes that can help with this explanation. *The first of these is the decline of trust.* There are good reasons for this trend, and it is useful to examine them if we are to have any hope of restoring trust—something that needs to be done.

The second of these is the irrational fear of a threat to the economy that has already been virtually eliminated: Communism. While the West rejoices in the collapse of the Soviet Union and the end of the Cold War, we persist with a fear that free enterprise will be undermined from within if the welfare state is allowed to expand or, as some would have it, allowed to exist at all. The problem is that work is slowly but surely being taken over by machines. That means that the economy's chief tool for distributing goods to people—employment—is becoming less effective every year. If we persist with the idea that sharing is bad because it is tantamount to Communism, then we are headed for a crisis.

The third of these is the contamination of public information with propaganda and random noise. This problem has its roots in economics as much as any other cause. We will expose those roots and trace them to the full flower of the disinformation economy. I will suggest some solutions, but that must wait until later in this book.

2.1 Black Socks

The Chicago White Sox baseball team lost the World Series in 1919. Some of the players on that team took money from gamblers to lose on purpose. It was the most scandalous thing that has ever happened in the nearly 200 year history of the sport. The reaction of the baseball establishment was swift and furious. Judge Kenesaw Mountain Landis banned the accused players from the sport for life. Because of these events, the game lost one of its greatest all-time players, Shoeless Joe Jackson. Why? What was the big deal?

The answer has a lot to do with financial markets. Almost all financial products depend on a promise made by one party to another to do something in the future if the other party does something now. This could be the borrower's promise to pay the loan back to the lender plus interest. It could be the insurance company's promise to pay a claim if the policy holder suffers from an insured event. It could be the bank's promise to give the depositor's money back when asked. It could be the credit card company's promise to pay a merchant for the card holder's purchase or its promise that the card holder will be able to use the card to buy something in a distant land from a complete stranger. The whole system depends on trust. No trust, and all these transactions become very hard to do, or impossible.

The Chicago Black Sox threatened the public's trust in the game of baseball. If you don't believe the athletes are trying to win, you will lose interest in the outcome. You certainly won't fork out the ticket price and waste a day at the stadium if you think the whole thing is fixed. You won't bother watching it on TV, and the advertisers won't bother paying the network for commercial spots during the game. That is why Judge Landis had to be so severe, and why the punishments had to be so public. He had to send a message that everyone would hear.

21st Century trust

If public opinion surveys are anything to go by, we have become a lot less trustful of authority figures in recent times. Politicians have always been looked at suspiciously in democratic societies, but this suspicion that they are putting their own interests first has been replaced by a sense of dead certainty. We do not trust our politicians. Normally, this conclusion would lead voters to change the party in government and let the other team have a go for a while. The trouble is that we don't trust the opposition, either. Who do we turn to?

The trust problem has become very widespread. We lose faith in religious institutions when they fail to protect the children in their care and everyone finds out about it. We lose faith in the press when the most outrageous lies are peddled as information-entertainment. The line between entertainment and fact has become blurry.

Slowly but surely, this sickness has affected financial markets, too. It was always a risk, given the importance of trust there. The things that used to give us faith in financial institutions have been gradually eroded or blasted to pieces. These things include bigness, greed and transparency, mutually assured destruction, and fear of punishment. As you'll see in a moment, none of these are working so well any more.

Bigness

Lions don't try to eat elephants. They are too big. Bigness means safety. Big banks used to be especially safe, for two reasons. First, like the elephant, they were too big to be eaten by a smaller bank and they never went in the ocean so there was no danger from sharks.

Second, the government would never let them fail because of the collateral damage that would cause. This is the other side to bigness— the many people who depend on you will protect you.

These reasons are very logical, and they were valid for a very long time, but not now. Lehman Brothers was too big to fail. It was an elephant and knew it. It felt safe. It felt safe the way that a racing car driver does when he has crash insurance. The insurance prompts him to drive faster and more recklessly. This is called moral hazard. We will talk about it later to explain why Communism failed.

The elephant, feeling very safe, decides it would be amusing to go swimming with sharks in the ocean. A gambler, knowing that the government will pay his tab, racks up a bigger and bigger debt at the casino.

One day, the sharks work out how to eat something as big as an elephant. Perhaps the orcas help them out. The same day, the gambler owes more money to the casino than the government can pay. The next day, we have a Global Financial Crisis.

Greed and transparency

Lehman Brothers were foolish. That's not going to happen every day. Financial people are not usually foolish. They are hard, practical people. Their behaviour is safe in one way because it is predictable. They do what they do because of greed. You can work out what they will do in any situation by following the money. They'll chose the option that makes them the most money. You could set your watch by it. Surely we can trust in greed?

The good news is that greed remains as powerful a motivator as ever. The new millennium has not tarnished greed's star. It is as clear as ever what people would like to achieve, but at the same time many high risk, high reward financial strategies have come to have unintended consequences.

Financial markets and financial products have become very complicated. It is not at all transparent how they work, and what might flow from one type of event or another. We now have products called derivatives that can be bought and sold on financial markets. They are called derivatives because they derive their value from changes in the value of something else. One simple type of derivative is a call option. I can use my call option to buy a share of company IBM at a future date at a price that is set now. There are put options, too, that let me sell a share of company BHP at a future date at a price set now.

One of the nice things about these options is their flexibility. I don't have to exercise them. I don't have to buy or sell the share when the time comes, I just have the option. If the price on the day is right, I will buy or sell, but if not, I won't. Another nice feature of the put option is that I don't have to own the share in BHP on the day I buy the option. I just have to make sure I own it by the time the exercise date rolls around. More generally you can sell, for future delivery, shares you don't own now. This is called short-selling. It's a little risky because once you've sold a stock short, you will have to buy it in order to fulfil your contract. However, when you do this you can get caught out if the price goes the wrong way.

These are just the simplest derivatives, built on stocks and bonds. There are also derivatives that are built on other derivatives, and further derivatives built on these meta-derivatives, and so on. There is virtually no limit to how tall this house of cards can be built.

One especially fascinating type of derivative is a credit default swap (CDS). This is a type of insurance contract and also a type of wager. You can use a CDS to insure yourself against some event happening. If the event happens, the person you contract with must pay your "insurance" claim. Here's the trick. A real insurance company will only let you insure something you own. The insurable event must happen to you before you can claim. However, there is no such constraint on a CDS. You can insure yourself against an event that happens to someone else. You could even insure yourself against someone else getting a payout from a different CDS.

If you tried to draw a diagram of all the contractual links that were created since CDSs first started, it would look like a diagram of all the page references in the world-wide web. It has become, as we used to say in a different age, like a can of worms. The main feature of a can of worms is that everything is connected to everything else.

What good is greed as a roadmap when you can't tell what road you're on?

Mutual destruction

The instinct for self-preservation is very strong in humans. There was a time when you could rely on someone else's preservation instinct to protect you, too. No one would detonate a bomb on a plane because that would kill them too. If only you could still rely on that logic.

This type of logic has been used in financial markets, too. People were happy to take the advice of rich investment advisers because if that advice was wrong, the adviser would lose even more money. It was a version of the doctrine of Mutually Assured Destruction (MAD) that guided so much of the thinking in Washington and Moscow during the Cold War. They won't attack us because if they did, we would destroy them. Surprisingly, this MAD doctrine actually worked, keeping the Cold War from getting hot.

But as you're probably realising, it is a different world now from the one I grew up in. We can no longer put any faith in Mutually Assured Destruction, at least in the financial world. We have seen global investment banks go broke because of rogue traders who didn't seem to care that they were destroying their company, and its clients. We have seen investment advisers tell their clients to buy securities that they were themselves selling because they were duds.

Punish the wind

Economics has recognised for a long time that when Aretha reaches an agreement with Betsy, sometimes Carol is affected in a bad way. There is not very much that Carol can do about this, because she is not a party to the contract. This is called an externality. For example, Aretha might be interviewing Betsy live on the TV news. Carol might be visible in the background picking her nose, unaware of the filming. The next thing you know, all of Carol's friends see her picking her nose on national television. If Betsy was talking about something boring, like economics say, then the footage of Carol might become the story.

There are lots of externalities in financial markets, particularly when big companies are involved. If a car company goes broke because the stock market crashed, then all its workers lose their jobs—even if they never bought or sold a single share. If the executives of an insurance company make bad choices, the policy holders may lose their coverage. If the government has to bail out that company, then every taxpayer would wind up paying for those executives' mistakes.

The bottom line is that it is becoming more common that business leaders who make expensive mistakes are not the ones who face the consequences. This brings back the problem of moral hazard. Governments should be thinking about how to rein in that problem, rather than how to make the regulations even looser.

Compounding this problem is the one I mentioned before about transparency. If a fog of derivatives makes it impossible to know who is responsible, how effective is the threat of punishment?

2.2 First World problems

If you are reading this story now, you probably speak English. You know how to read. You have enough spare time to read, and you have enough surplus income to buy books or download them on a computer. If you don't, perhaps your parents do. Chances are, you live in what was called the first world, now the developed world.

Planet Earth is our world, and there is only one, but on the surface of this planet there are said to be three great collections of people. The differences in the material standard of life of these groups are so great that they might as well live in different worlds, or perhaps in the same world at different eras.

Three worlds

The first world, where I live and you probably live, comprises the people of Europe, North America, East Asia and a few islands in the Pacific Ocean that were settled by the English. This collection of people is called "first" because it is the first that we think of. In fact, most of the time it is the only people we think of. We see our friends and neighbours, who are pretty much like us, and we assume that everyone is like us. We tend to think that the problems we have are the same problems that everyone has.

Mankind's historical problems—the ones that have been solved by farming, machines, money and all that—are problems we don't have any more in the first world. Because of these successes, problems like hunger, disease, anarchy, backwardness and poverty seem to be problems that no longer exist. We think this because we don't know anyone who has these problems and we don't go to the places where such people live.

The third world is where such people live. Where lawlessness is prevented, it is mainly prevented by brutal dictators. These dictators and their chums have all the money and everyone else is poor. These places don't have good roads, schools or hospitals for the common folk. Their houses often don't have electricity or running water. In one way, the people of the third world have the same problems people had centuries ago, before we had all those clever ideas.

In another way, the people of the third world are worse off than primitive humans. These people know all about the automobile, computers and electricity. They just can't have these things. They don't have anything to trade for them. They know what they want because they can see it on television.

By now you may be thinking that something is missing. Whatever happened to the second world, if there are three? The second world has been practically written out of the history books. It is seldom mentioned. The reason for this is interesting, and worth spending a little time on.

The second world was invented, by accident, by a strange German man who wound up living in England. His surname is the same as Groucho, Chico, Harpo and Zeppo. He invented a different way of doing economics than the one you see in the first world. Our system is capitalism, which is the main way of organising things nowadays. This alternative system was called communism. The second world is the collection of countries that adopted it as their economic system. The two largest examples of this approach are found in Russia and China, as well as their satellite countries. Several other countries have experimented with it, too.

The main difference between capitalism and communism is about who owns what. In capitalism there is such a thing as private property. In particular, the two most valuable types of things to own—land and machines—are owned by individual people, and these people are pretty much free to do what they like with this property. The people who own machines, the capitalists, have a lot of power over the workers and unemployed people who would like to be workers. The people who own land, the rentiers as they are called, have a lot of power over people who need somewhere to live and unemployed people who would like to work on someone else's farm.

Karl Marx didn't like this. He felt it was unfair. In communism, which he preferred, land and machines are owned by the Government, which was also known as the collective. The surplus from farming and using machines was meant to be shared among the workers in an equal way. When the economy did well, everyone was better off. Not just in an average way, but every person was better off. This emphasis on sharing was a point of difference to capitalism. We will return to it.

There was a contest of ideas between capitalism and communism during the 1900s. This contest was not just some high school debate. It was a full-blooded confrontation between the countries that adopted communism and those that adopted capitalism. This was called the Cold War. It was not called the Cold War because Russia, where it started, is a cold place. It was a Cold War because very few people got killed. Although it was full of menace and danger, even the possible destruction of all three worlds, Armageddon didn't happen.

It is generally thought that the Cold War ended in 1991, and that capitalism won. After that, most of the second world became part of the first world, so now we just have a developed world and a developing world. This is a nicer way to put it than to say the successful world and the failing world. Like in school, when you fail a subject, they don't come right out and say it. Instead they say you are working toward being able to spell or do arithmetic. The third world is working toward being part of the first world—hence it is developing.

Why did communism fail?

If you were born after 1991, you may wonder what ever happened to communism and why the second world is never talked about. It is never talked about because the winners of the Cold War hope that the ideas of communism will go away. That is because they still represent a threat to the pure form of capitalism that we mistakenly believe that we have. Before talking about that threat, though, we must explain why communism didn't work in the 1980s.

The problem is called moral hazard. The communist state is like an insurance company that guarantees every worker will get enough money to live on. A good worker and a lazy one get the same reward. If you invent something really useful, the profit from this invention is taken by the state and given to everyone. The motivation to work hard or to innovate is weakened by this sharing idea. A person could do just as well being lazy and ignorant as by being diligent and clever. Many people, although not everyone, will slack off and take advantage of the opportunities to free-ride.

Some of the people who didn't want to slack off realised that they could do better for themselves if they moved to a capitalist country. This pattern of movement became prevalent before it was ruthlessly stamped out by the communist countries. It was called the Brain Drain. Why did the communist countries need to stamp it out? Because it was leading to a second big problem for insurance companies, called adverse selection. If people could go and live where they liked, the sharing rule would encourage the smart overachievers to leave, while the lazy incompetents had equally strong reasons to stay. The communist country would unintentionally select the least desirable citizens to make up the future workforce.

The productivity of the entire economy can start to drop if enough smart people leave and dumb people take the easy option. The communist state tried to stop this behaviour, but the only way to do that, apart from resorting to capitalism and private property, is to get tough. People don't like it when the Government gets tough with them. They started off being lazy, but then they became resentful, too. The communist economies simply were not as productive or inventive as the capitalist economies, and that is why communism lost in the end.

Why might sharing be a bad idea?

When the communist countries lost the Cold War, a lot of selfish people concluded that their selfish feelings had been validated. The lesson they took from all of that was that communism was based on sharing and therefore sharing was a bad idea and selfishness was a good one. Sharing was not just a bad idea, but a *dangerous* one.

Ideas can be dangerous, you know. Even though they are just things that flit through your mind which have no colour or odour, they make people do things. Dangerous things. It's a bit like carbon dioxide—you can't see it but it's ruining the climate.

Why would the idea of sharing your own good fortune with less fortunate people be a bad idea? How could this idea harm you or your family? The answer to that is a bit complicated. It has to do with the problems with communism—moral hazard and adverse selection. Too much sharing, and people will lose their discipline. If they expect to be given food and shelter without effort, then they won't help to make food or shelter. Eventually no one will. So the story goes. I think even a six year old can see how ridiculous that story is once it's written out in plain language.

A time to share and a time not to

Mankind, as we have come to call ourselves, has gone through times of need and times of plenty. Long ago there were plenty of times of need and not many of plenty. More recently, the pockets of need are mostly found in the third world.

The solution to need is growth. If there are too many mouths to feed, grow more food. Work harder. Growth will be faster if people have strong incentives to think clever new thoughts and to spend long hours working. An incentive is just a reason to do something.

Sharing messes this all up because it disorients workers. It takes away these incentives to try hard. In times of need, when growth is required to solve the problem, a philosophy of wide-spread sharing can get in the way of a solution.

Things are different in a time of plenty. We don't actually know the solution to plenty. We tend not to see it as a problem, but it is. One thing is for sure, though. Growth is not the solution to plenty. In fact growth in times of plenty is a bit counterproductive.

Another thing is clear. In times of plenty the objections to sharing—

the lost incentives to work hard—don't really make sense any more. Perhaps sharing is an idea whose time hadn't come before the Cold War was over, but that time is coming now in the 21st century.

The unsharing economy

Machines have become extremely clever. Where once they could only do the jobs that people didn't want to do, now they can do jobs that people do want to do. Sadly, machines do many of these jobs much faster, cheaper, and with higher quality of service than a person could ever do. It is not just ditch-diggers that are being replaced by machines. Nowadays it is also lawyers, accountants, doctors and even some engineers. It is foreseeable that even artists and composers of music will be competing with machines.

These machines are creating plenty of everything, but getting it out to people has become a bigger problem than ever before. The reason is that the capitalist method of getting products to people depends on the idea that people have jobs. Capitalists use the work that people do to make things to sell and pay the workers a wage. People use their wages to buy the things they need and want.

However, if capitalists use the work that machines do to make things to sell, they don't need to pay the workers a wage, and people don't have anything with which to buy the things they need. At first this is a problem for the workers, but after a while it becomes a problem for the capitalists, too, because if nobody buys the things they make, they don't have as much money to buy what they need, either.

The capitalists' problem seems a long way off. It is true that some workers will always be needed, but the workers that cost the least live in the third world. Also these people have the most urgent needs for food, shelter and all that. The emerging pattern is that the source of labour and the demand for products is shifting to the third world, while the capitalists of the first world continue more or less as before. The workers of the first world have suddenly been economised out of the loop. They are no longer needed by this economic system. But they still vote.

2.3 Information gone bad

It's time to consider how well voting and democracy are serving us in the information age. To be honest, we are experiencing a type of breakdown. People don't seem able to get the laws or decisions that they want, even though they can vote for whoever they like. There are many possible reasons for that.

It's fairly obvious that voters are not always making the best choices for themselves. This is not an insight. It is just a restatement of the problem. The question is why? Part of the answer is that there is a problem with the way voters inform themselves about what is going on.

There is a certain irony that in the information age we can't easily work out which way is up. I hear the phrase "information age" quite a lot. I think many people who use it aren't really sure what they mean by it, so let's begin by nailing down what exactly makes this age the information one.

Thanks to computers, digital media and telecommunication networks, it is possible now to copy information and send it to many people at nearly zero cost. That means that if I have a nugget of truth, I can share it very easily, and many people can benefit from it. The downside is that if I have a nugget of falsehood, I can do the same thing very easily, and many people may become quite confused as a result. That is one feature of the information age.

Another feature is that some ideas are now very valuable. We have reached a stage of industrial development in which the only truly unique capital items are ideas. If you have the idea, you can build the machine, cure the disease, unlock the secret and make a fortune. If the idea belongs to you and you can keep it secret, you can get someone else to build the machine, mass produce the vaccine, or manufacture the running shoes for a pittance while you bank the royalties.

So here we have two candidate theories (among many others) about why the information age is not living up to its potential. First, we are living in a disinformation age—one where new skills will be necessary to filter the noise out to perceive the signal accurately. Second, people who know what's really going on have strong incentives not to tell you.

To map out this landscape, I will begin by reminding you about how democracy was meant to work. Then I will examine the way that people inform themselves about politics, ie the news. After that I will talk about disinformation, which is also called propaganda. Then I will talk about the problems that can occur when someone knows something that you don't. How did these issues come to threaten our democratic rights? It is hard to be definitive, but I offer a few possible answers.

A thumbnail sketch of democracy

Most of the first world has adopted a democratic form of government. That means that the people who live in a country choose the people who govern them, and they are chosen from among the population of normal everyday people. Leaders have to face the voters every few years, and when there is a change of leadership it is done peacefully.

Many of the important decisions of government are made by smart people who know what they're doing, but who are not elected. These are called bureaucrats. The bureaucrats can't run amuck because they have to obey the elected leaders.

The idea is that the politicians are good at knowing what people want, while the bureaucrats are good at getting things done. The citizens elect the politicians, who tell the bureaucrats to do what the people want, and then the bureaucrats do it.

This system has turned out to be popular because, when leaders don't do what people want, it gives people the chance to elect different ones. If the bureaucrats aren't up to the job, then the politicians get rid of them and hire better ones.

As we will see, democracy is not a foolproof system. The weak link is the voter. If the voters make silly group decisions on who to elect or if they don't know what they want, then things can go awry.

A thumbnail sketch of the news

One of the marvels of the modern world, the newspaper, is now on the brink of being obsolete. Herr Gutenburg, the inventor of the printing press, would have been astounded to learn that it was possible to print tens of thousands of copies of 50 page documents every single day containing long, complex stories and pictures that change every day, and that the whole thing was relevant to the important decisions we all make on who will govern us and how. Until you've seen it, you simply would not believe it.

Now, of course, in the information age, there are faster and more efficient ways to spread the information and disinformation that these newspapers present. Some of them, like the television news, are not really as effective at delivering the information. There's so little time to convey the substance of any story, and those stories are biased towards topics that have arresting images. Because broadcast media are synchronous (meaning you must experience it when it is broadcast or not at all) there is an enormous amount of repetition in order to make sure you don't miss anything unimportant. Some people prefer it because it doesn't tax their brains too much, and they find the repetition reassuring.

Others, like the internet, have great potential because, like the newspaper they are asynchronous (meaning you can enjoy it when you want, not when the network says) but unlike the newspaper they don't require massive printing presses or a fleet of trucks and a galaxy of newsstands.

Leaving the delivery mechanism aside, have you ever stopped to wonder what the news actually is? To most people, it's a collection of stories about things that are going on now. We like to think it is different from fiction in that it is true. Because of this truth feature, and because it's just happened, we accept the fact that the news is not told in the beautiful style of *1001 Arabian Nights* or Homer's *Iliad*. It had to be compiled in a hurry and the reporters couldn't make stuff up, so the endings tend to be a bit messy.

The reason people put up with the ugliness of the news, as a collection of short stories, is that it is important to their decisions about what to do next. There are actually two distinct types of news: fact and opinion.

Fact news can be quite useful in ordinary life. Let us imagine that you have to make an important decision, like where to go for dinner on an important date. There are many restaurants to choose from, but you don't know what they're like. If you choose a dud, your date may form a bad impression of you, so the stakes are high. You can't go and try them all, because that would be expensive and the date is next Saturday. Fortunately, there is a section of the newspaper that contains restaurant reviews. You can read it and make a well-informed choice.

There's more to life than eating dinner, and fact news can help with a lot of these other challenges, too. Whenever you need to make a decision but the outcome is uncertain, there is a possibility that news can give you the information you need to make a better choice.

News as opinion

Something called opinion is also found in newspapers. It is usually an opinion about politics. Now, clearly, opinions are not facts and should not be confused with them. A "news-paper" should, strictly speaking, confine itself to facts. However, opinion can also be useful if it is done in the right way.

Opinion, or comment, is an interpretation of facts that can shed light on the values of politicians and the competence of bureaucrats. The right way of doing opinion is to make sure that the "facts" actually are true, that they are relevant to the interpretation that is being given, and that all of the relevant facts are included.

Why do we care about the values of politicians and the competence of bureaucrats? We elect politicians to direct the bureaucrats to achieve our goals. Politicians have a lot of freedom once they get into their jobs, so it is important that they have the same values that we do. If not, they might direct the bureaucrats to do the wrong thing. It can be very easy to pretend to have a value that they don't really have, so the small gestures and actions of politicians need to be carefully watched to make sure they mean what they say.

Bureaucrats are not elected, but rather they are chosen by other bureaucrats and politicians. Bureaucrats basically do everything in government. Unlike the politicians, they need to know what they're doing. They need to be skilful and diligent. As long as the politicians are trying to do the right thing and the bureaucrats are smart enough to get it done, the government will achieve our goals. If the bureaucrats are incompetent, we need to find out about that pretty quickly. That is why we need the opinion pages in the newspaper.

What I just said about the opinion pages was based on the idea that opinion is done in the right way. If it is done in the wrong way, it is just propaganda. Listen to enough propaganda, and you are flying a P-51 upside down into the Bermuda Triangle until you run out of gas and crash into the sea.

You will recall that opinion is only useful if several conditions are satisfied. At the risk of being tedious, I will repeat them.

1 The facts that are interpreted by the opinion must be true and verifiable.

2 They must be relevant to the interpretation that is given.

3 All relevant facts must be presented.

4 Where something important is unknown, that should be made clear, so that we know to seek further information before making a decision.

It so happens that these rules are nearly the same as the rules that apply to expert witnesses in court. A court of law is a serious place, and judges can get tough with witnesses who misbehave.

It so happens that these rules are also very similar to the rules that apply to scientists who are trying to get their work published in good journals. Scientific journals are serious places, and peer reviewers can get tough with professional scientists who misbehave.

The weak point of our entire democratic system is that the court of public opinion is a three ring circus, where showmanship is prized above truthfulness. Nobody gets tough with misbehavers. In fact they are often rewarded handsomely if they are entertaining enough.

Disinformation

I mentioned that we are living in what you could call the disinformation age because the radio signal of truth is being overwhelmed by the static of irrelevant material and downright untruth. It is natural to assign some blame to the promoters of this static, which I refer to as propaganda here. However, we would be missing something important if we didn't ask how modern conditions are supporting the proliferation of this confusion.

The term "propaganda" was made famous by an evil genius who used it to promote a now discredited social movement. We have something like it today, but we call it advertising when it is applied to persuading ordinary people to do silly things. It is called lobbying when it is applied to convincing politicians to act against the public interest.

The enemy of propaganda is science. For a heroic period that lasted from the 16th century until fairly recently, science was used to great effect to expose and defeat self-interested lies and advance the public interest.

Unfortunately, the enemy of science is propaganda. For a less heroic period that began in my lifetime and, at the time of writing has not yet ended, propaganda was used to great effect to make a large group of voters doubt science. According to this myth, science is not an absolute truth, but only one possible interpretation of things.

Whether you choose to adopt science or not is a matter of personal choice. I should be free to choose to paint my house biblical black rather than eco-friendly green. The same goes for which theory of natural history is taught in my children's school. I should be able to decide whether it is Darwin's evolution or a fairy tale.

We are seeing a fragmentation of the consensus view of the world, which is related to a long-term decline in civic engagement and what you might call social capital among ordinary people. As a result, people agree with each other less and less about what are our main problems and how we should fix them. The causes of this trend are complicated. Sociologist Robert Putnam, in a wide-ranging book about bowling, identified a few candidate causes:

- Growing pressures of time and money within families leave people with little capacity to engage in civic activities
- The rise of suburbs, with longer commutes to work and larger physical separation between family homes
- The isolating effects of electronic entertainment, especially television
- The passing of the pre baby-boom generation whose first-hand experience of World War II instilled a commitment to social engagement.

This fragmentation works against the scientific method. People don't have to confront people who hold views they disagree with, so there is no need to overcome the cognitive dissonances that have become so common. When you hold a view that is contradicted by reality, there is likely no one in your circle to warn you, because they are likely all suffering from the same delusion. Thus, when actual reality reasserts its dominance—well, you won't read about it in all the papers, but if it happens to you, you will feel it.

Is there an economic angle in all of this idealism? Consider how the news gets to us, who controls those distribution channels and what messages they might want us to hear. News is transmitted through networks of various sorts, be they newspapers, radio or television stations, or the world wide web. These transmission systems experience something we call network effects, which means that a new subscriber is better off joining a large network than a small one. This means that the big networks get bigger and the small ones stay that way.

The owners of these large transmission platforms had a lot of market power. For whatever reason, these owners chose to use that power to project a coherent view of society. That reason may be related to moral choices of those individuals. Perhaps, these owners were beholden to advertisers who feared that highly radical opinions would hurt their sales. It might have been something more prosaic, such as the fact that broadcast channels were scarce, so you couldn't transmit very many different points of view.

Whatever the explanation, this situation didn't last. Technology caught up with these oligarchs. Clever engineers worked out how to squeeze a lot more TV channels into the radio spectrum. They worked out how to broadcast TV over cables, which could host hundreds of channels. Then, as if things couldn't get any worse for an honest abuser of monopoly power, the internet was invented. Personally, I blame the United States Air Force for this calamity. The internet was their idea, after all.

On one hand, it was a momentous victory for competition, which we would all normally applaud. However, this development created the conditions where people could isolate themselves and a handful of fellow-travellers in a series of micro-villages. Imagine that each of these was a voting district. No one will ever know how many voters there are in each of these micro-districts, but the micro-villagers can make themselves look big by speaking very loudly. It is another form of malapportionment: these echo chambers have become very modern versions of the rotten boroughs of England. All of a sudden, every fringe viewpoint demands to be given equal time in the public policy debate.

Information that is not symmetric

I noted earlier that an essential feature of the information age is that knowledge is power. That being so, you might think twice about sharing what you know with others. When I know something you don't, an economist would say that there is an information asymmetry. Economists have recently recognised that information asymmetry is an important explanation for all sorts of features of our modern world.

We can get an intuitive feel for some of these features by focusing on a sales transaction. If I am selling you something or buying from you, I may get a good deal at your expense because of the knowledge that I have and you don't. For example, I may know that the second-hand car I'm selling you is a lemon, but because you don't know that you might pay too much or fail to do what you should have done—buy a different car from someone else. My gain is your loss, but overall the transaction is a zero sum game.

Looking beyond the immediate transaction, you and I will each learn something from the experience and act differently next time. These behavioural changes are also a consequence of information asymmetry, but they will ensure that it is no longer a zero sum game.

You will become more wary of knowledgeable traders. You will refuse to take part in some trades that you might previously have made.

You will require a bigger and more certain benefit before you will go into a trade. In brief, society will be worse off because vastly fewer mutually beneficial trades will take place.

The problem could be mitigated if a knowledgeable trader was willing to share her valuable knowledge and reduce the information asymmetry, but she has no incentive to do that. That is what she learned from the first transaction.

How does advertising or political advocacy fit into this picture? We pretend that advertising was created as a vehicle for sellers to inform potential buyers of the virtues of their product. The less cynical among us may think that political advocacy was created in order for earnest statesmen to let the people know about the great social achievements that would be possible if their policies were enacted. This is the view that advertising and political advocacy are valuable to the buyer because they inform—they reduce the information asymmetry.

Years of experience of buyer's remorse has convinced many of us that advertising is valuable principally to the seller because it persuades. In other words, it increases the information asymmetry.

From the outset, it is not plausible that advertising is supposed to reduce an information asymmetry. Doing that would empower the buyer at the expense of the seller. A seller would have no incentive to give away her valuable knowledge, even if advertising cost her nothing.

However advertising is not free. It is expensive for the seller. It is an investment in an intangible asset that we might call "brand equity", reputation, or "political capital." The seller must make a profit on that advertising investment, either by increasing volume or price. The political donor must get a return on that advocacy investment by securing valuable rights from the government.

Now this analysis seems to turn the conventional view of advertising on its head. Are we sure it's correct? If it's right that advertising's true purpose is to persuade, even mislead, then two questions come to mind. First, how does the innocent act of informing people about your product create winners and losers? Second, if advertising is completely truthful, how can it make the buyer worse off?

Regarding the first question, advertising is designed to focus attention on the advertiser's product to the exclusion competing products. It might well be the case that the competing products are virtually identical in all important dimensions, but advertising creates an availability bias in favour of the advertised product. The similarity of competing products is the vital information that advertising obscures.

Regarding the second question, it is clear that the provision of false information can increase asymmetry. If I tell you something that I know isn't true and you believe it, then I could exploit that incorrect belief. Are there cases, though, where the provision of true information can increase asymmetry? Arguably, yes. In the example just given, advertising can make the buyer myopic without imparting any misinformation. Occupying the buyer's attention with irrelevant, but true, details can distract him from making diligent inquiries and discovering, say, some defect or safety problem with the product.

Having reached the view that advertising increases the information asymmetry between sellers and buyers, it remains to consider what can or should be done about it. The existing prohibitions against false advertising are necessary, but not sufficient. As we have just noted, true advertising can also mislead. Here are some further suggestions:

1   Levy each industry's advertising expenditure to support published consumer research into product performance in that industry.

2   Prohibit claims in advertising that are not falsifiable. Many advertising statements are persuasive to some degree without actually making a claim that is able to be shown to be either true or false. Since the statement cannot be falsified, then no legal action can be taken against the advertiser. This suggested prohibition would put the onus on advertisers to demonstrate the truth of their claims, rather than on consumer advocates to demonstrate their falseness. This arrangement would better match the required effort with the financial resources available to support it.

We have now seen that the information asymmetry that helps to keep us from understanding what is going on is durable. Many interest groups are working hard to increase it, under the guise of activities that would seem to be breaking it down. Freedom of speech provisions in the laws and constitutions of many lands would normally help to make information more symmetric. Yet these provisions are often used to give the wealthy and powerful a bigger megaphone so they can out-shout contrary viewpoints.

So, are we better informed in the information age?

We have shown ourselves to be vulnerable to propaganda. We've come a long way as a species by being smart and learning, but suddenly and inexplicably we seem willing to entertain ideas that have been proven wrong ages ago. We are sceptical about uncomfortable truths even when reputable scientists vouch for them. One could say that in a collective sense we behave stupidly. Not because we are stupid ourselves, but because other people are stupid and we must anticipate their moves.

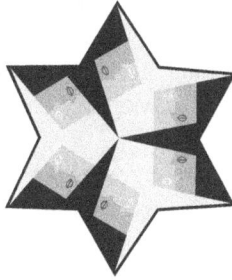

3

WHY GROWTH WON'T SAVE US

More than we might realise, the wagon of humanity's hopes for the future is hitched to the star of growth. We are trained to think that we are better off when the world economy grows. It seems to mean more of everything for everyone. We are trained to think that more of everything is good for us. Is it, though?

The notion that more is better rests on a hidden assumption, called free disposal. If I have more stuff, I can't be worse off than if I had less stuff, because in a pinch I could always get rid of some of it. But if I had less stuff, it's not so clear how I would move to a position of having more. You see, this logic depends on the idea that it doesn't cost anything to get rid of any stuff I don't want. If I had to pay to get rid of it, then the decision whether to have more or less would become a more difficult one.

When the human footprint on Earth was so small that no one noticed it, the ecosystem was our rubbish tip, and it didn't change very much when we dumped a load. Clearly that is no longer so, and the idea of free disposal is as ludicrous as the idea of a free lunch. Inescapably, that means that 'more is better' is no longer a universal rule. What does that imply about the virtue of growth?

Putting the propaganda aside, growth is important because it is very useful politically. It can solve a lot of problems for a government. It can take people's minds off the lack of sharing that is going on. If everyone can have a bit more each year because of growth, it doesn't matter so much that some people get more than others. It helps to keep government stable and democracy on the rails.

The bad news that I must break to you in this chapter is that global economic growth is running out of steam, and therefore humanity's aspirations that depend on it will not be met. There are two reasons for this.

The first is that we are running out of the inputs that growth requires. This problem is fairly well known and much discussed in the news and other media. Nevertheless I will take you through the history of this idea and test a notion that has given some commentators comfort. That notion is that mankind's ingeniousness will allow us to do a loaves and fishes type trick to feed an ever growing population with less and less of all inputs.

The second is that we are losing the individual desire for growth. This idea is pretty startling. It runs contrary to what you are likely to read in other books, and yet there is some good evidence for it. I will take you through that evidence and consider what it might mean for our future.

3.1 The dismal side of the force

You may have heard that the Earth is warming up and that industrial activity is the cause. This is one of those inconvenient truths that are often denied. It is also the latest echo of an idea that started to be taken seriously when a killjoy named Thomas Malthus first noticed it.

That idea is that population grows faster than the ability to support it, leading to a cycle of boom and bust. When technology improves and we get better at growing food, it does not solve the boom and bust problem. It makes it even worse. The booms last longer and population soars to even greater heights only to crash harder when the food is insufficient to feed everyone. These crashes take the form of warfare, starvation, destruction of the machinery of the economic system, and prolonged misery until the population has been reduced far enough that a growth phase can begin again.

If this idea is still valid today, it means that the sustainability of business as usual for the world is in serious doubt. A great many well informed people say flat out that it is unsustainable. There are people who hold a contrary view, and do so loudly, but their contrariness is often rooted in self-interest.

My purpose in this chapter is not to adjudicate in this disagreement, but rather to map out the history of the idea that economic growth has hard limits imposed by the scarcity of all types of inputs. These inputs include land, fossil fuels, ocean fisheries, forests, clean air, drinkable water and temperate zones with good rainfall where farming can take place. We are becoming pot-bound within the confines of our planet. Will growth slow down or will we crash into the barrier at high speed?

The dismal science

Economics is called the dismal science. Some quite rightly question the claim that economics is in fact a science, given the amount of propaganda that is espoused by prominent economists and people in the public eye who claim to know economics.

Dismal it is, however. The happy ending, according to one of the most famous economists, is that we all die. The tag "dismal" came about because Malthus predicted that the human population would always eventually outstrip the available food, leading to a crisis and mass death. More recently, his predictions have been refined by some good economic work, which we will examine in this chapter.

Malthus noticed that when unrestrained, the population of any animal, including humans, will double in size every few years. The time the population takes to double is approximately the same when the population is 150 as when it is 25 million. This phenomenon is called exponential growth.

For most animals this is not really a problem. For example, an exponential outbreak of rabbits will be followed by an exponential outbreak of foxes. The foxes will halt the exponential growth of the rabbit population and then the depleted rabbit stocks will lead to starvation of the excess foxes. This would be unfortunate for the starving foxes, but it would not threaten the stability of the ecosystem in the long term.

For human beings it is really a problem. We are the apex predator on the planet, so there will be no exponential outbreak of flesh-eating aliens to check our "progress." However, unlike the foxes, we don't starve when we run out of rabbits to eat. We just eat something else instead. And when that runs out too, we just find something else to eat—maybe whale meat from halfway around the world. You see, unlike the foxes, we can go anywhere in the world and do whatever we like.

Exponential population growth means exponential demand for all the things necessary for our lives. Malthus focused on food, but you could equally think of drinking water, uncontaminated land, and even clean air to breathe. In his day, which was in the late 1700s and early 1800s, there probably seemed to be plenty of clean air (except perhaps in London) and no shortage of drinking water as it rains so much in England.

Sticking with food, then, the issue is whether its production can keep pace with an exponentially growing number of mouths to feed. At first, you might think that doubling the population will double the number of workers who can sow and reap, bake bread and sell it in a shop. But this rosy thought bubble bursts when you consider that almost all production functions have diminishing returns to scale. That's a bit of economist speak for the notion that when you double the amount of input you get less than double the amount of output.

In the particular case of food, the diminishing returns to scale come about because one of the most critical inputs, arable land, was limited by the fact that England is on an island. So, exponential population growth coupled with diminishing returns to food production means there will be a problem down the track.

But surely, with all that time to get ready for the crunch time, people would stop having children before the food runs out? Perhaps. It is a possibility, but we need to respect the seriousness of the challenge that exponential growth poses. Here is an example of that challenge.

When the human colony in an area is 100 people living in a forest clearing, you might expect the size of the group to grow by 10% every 10 years. At the end of a decade there would be 110 people in the tribe. If the food supply didn't grow, either 10 people could go hungry or everyone could eat a bit less and everyone would be basically fine. At the end of the next decade, there would be 121 people in the tribe. If the food supply still didn't grow, it would be time to do something about the rate of new arrivals because everyone could not carry on consuming 17% less than subsistence rations.

When the human colony in an area is 1 million people living in a city that also experiences 10% population growth every 10 years, a hiccup in food supply would be far more serious. Suddenly, the city leaders have to decide whether to let 100,000 people go hungry or ask every one of 1.1 million people to tighten their belts by 9%. Undoubtedly, some of those 1.1 million people will refuse to cooperate so others will need to endure starvation rations. The hungry won't take it sitting down. One hundred thousand dissidents can cause a lot of trouble.

A strategy of wait and see might work for the tribe in the jungle, but it would be a recipe for disaster for the big city. Malthus was in the recipe for disaster camp. While noting that it was possible for married couples to marry later in life or to be abstinent in order to control population growth, he felt that such restraint was the exception rather than something you could rely on. Therefore the future did not look rosy to him.

Modern limits to growth

As far as I know, Thomas Malthus did not have a computer. Even if he did, he would not have had much useful data about national accounts, industrial output, pollution, or even world population to plug into it. For this reason he was not able to fully explore the consequences of his idea.

Two hundred and six years after he was born, another group of dismal scientists calling themselves the Club of Rome undertook a computer modelling task that did fully explore these consequences. They were, of course, aided by the invention of the digital computer and the compilation of these national accounts, scientific and demographic data. They published their results in a short book entitled "The Limits to Growth."

In many ways, this was an impressive piece of work. They saw the entire world, embracing all its biomes and its economies, as a unified dynamical system. They carefully traced through hundreds of feedback loops between human population, human economic activity, consumption of natural resources and production of pollutants, birth rates and death rates.

They calibrated their dynamic model using measurements of lead contamination in the Greenland ice cap, waste heat generation in Los Angeles, nuclear waste, fish production in Lake Ontario, oxygen content of the Baltic Sea, flows of mercury and DDT, nutrition and life expectancy, and many other indicators of economic "progress" and its effect on the quantity and quality of life.

Once they assembled and calibrated this model they were able to explore possible futures for the world and evaluate the impact on those futures of certain policy changes. This model recognised that many of the data points and relationships were subject to uncertainty, so they simulated many possible futures to establish a range of possibilities.

For the first time, it was possible to see whether Malthus was right or not under 20th century conditions taking account of the modern, post-industrial economy. What they found was rather depressing. It seemed that Malthus had been right all along. More importantly, though, they could see the world as a huge machine with policy dials that could be twiddled in ways that would make the difference between a soft landing or a severe crash.

There was no doubting that growth was limited. The only questions were when would the crunch arrive, what might it look like when it did, and what could governments do to soften the blow?

It works in theory, but does it work in fact?

Obviously, everyone sat up and took notice of the Club of Rome's work and we all lived happily ever after. Well, not really. In typical fashion for economists, there was a lot of nit-picking about the modelling work they did. Dynamic system modelling has come to be viewed in much the same way as we view airbags. These models are thought to injure as many people as they save.

Putting this in a slightly less facetious way, the obtuseness of complicated models can dispose them equally well to serve the needs of science or propaganda. How does an ordinary citizen evaluate what such models tell them?

Many people were inclined to disbelieve what the Club of Rome was saying, even though it was rather obvious that the world's natural resources are finite. The contrary theory was that mankind's ingeniousness would save us from the crunch. We would invent better ways to make things, to feed ourselves, to energise our machines so that we could continue to enjoy our lavish first world lifestyles, and so could everyone in the third world. We would do more with less through technology and there would be no need for belt-tightening.

These people weren't very clear about which specific technology would come to the rescue, because it hadn't been invented yet. (Still hasn't. For example, clean coal.) That didn't matter. Look at humanity's track record, they said. It is too impressive to discount the possibility of an ingenious escape.

When in doubt about a theoretical prediction (from a model, say), the best approach is to look at humanity's track record. This is called empirical science, and there is a lot to recommend it. In this case, we can legitimately ask what human history can tell us about our ability in past population crises to innovate our way out of them. This is precisely what two scholars, Peter Turchin and Sergey Nefedov, did in an ambitious empirical study entitled "Secular Cycles" published in 2009.

They compiled evidence of a particular cyclical pattern in the rise and fall of agrarian societies. This pattern involved more than just the demographic dynamics that Malthus focused on. It went further than the Club of Rome in that it takes account of the social structure (elites and commoners), the government and the way it is financed. Here is a rough sketch of the pattern.

Starting from a point where natural resources are in excess of current human requirements, population will grow until it approaches the carrying capacity of the area. At that point several changes start to alter society. There will be food shortages and too much labour relative to need. This will affect prices: food becoming more expensive and wages falling. The poorer parts of society will suffer higher mortality rates and lower reproduction, but this won't stabilise the growth.

The structure of society will respond to these price signals. Rural workers will relocate to the cities, where manufacturing will get a boost from the low price of labour and the concentration of the workforce. The elites, who own the land, get richer because rents rise while they don't need to pay their workers as much. The poor become more numerous and worse off. However, there is no revolution as long as the elites are united. They have the means to subdue the rabble and maintain order.

The real problem, from society's point of view, starts when the elites become too numerous to remain united. As a group, these elites will manage to extract all the available surplus that their realm will provide. However, as they have their own children, the number of princes, dukes, earls, barons and other aristocrats will increase—possibly in an exponential way. At some point, all the surplus in the kingdom will not be enough to support the whole aristocracy in the manner to which they have become accustomed. At that point, the elites will no longer be united. As a result, the government, which relies on the elites to fund its operations, will start to lose its ability to maintain order.

If this pattern is starting to sound a bit familiar that is because it has happened before. Turchin and Nefedov have meticulously documented each of these phases in Medieval England during the Plantagenet dynasty from 1150 to 1485, in early modern England during the Tudor and Stuart dynasties from 1485 to 1730, in medieval France from 1150 to 1450, in early modern France from 1450 to 1660, in the Roman republic from 350 to 30 BCE, in Rome from 30 BCE to the year 285, in Russia from 1460 to 1620, and in the Romanov dynasty from 1620 to 1922.

Among many clever historical methods, these authors used the discovery of coin hoards to mark and date periods of political instability. The idea is that in turbulent times, families will keep money 'under the mattress' so to speak. In fact they are more likely to hide it in the walls of their house or in the foundations. These coin hoards are intentionally hard to find, so when archaeologists dig them up, any direct link to the time they were stored may be lost. Luckily, though, coins can fairly easily be dated. A lot of coins actually have the date stamped on them. Even where they don't, historians can establish a date by referring to mint records or simply noting which King graces the coin with his profile.

So, how well did humanity invent its way out of the population crisis in the eight episodes studied in Secular Cycles? Poorly. In fact, we did not avert crisis in any of them. Population crashed each time. Societies disintegrated. Rebuilding took decades of hard work and suffering.

In reviewing that track record, we can take no comfort from the fact that it's all ancient history. The first episode mentioned in the book started in 350 BCE and the last one finished in 1922. We can't say that these were primitive societies that lack sophisticated science. They were societies much more like our own than we might be comfortable admitting.

There is a clue in this work about why science didn't save the Plantagenets or anyone else. This conflict between the elites over a shrinking per-baron surplus meant that the institutions that support science and the government bureaucracies that put good ideas into practice were becoming dysfunctional at precisely the point they were needed the most. The ideas may have been there, but there was no capacity to act on them.

Theory and observation suggest that Malthus' disturbing ideas still haunt us. Does it really need to be so? Perhaps we have not inquired deeply enough into the population dynamics that are at the root of this problem.

Some conjectured reasons for population explosion

You don't need a PhD in demographics to realise that the reason we have an out-of-control human population is that some people are having too many children. Why do they do that? Can't they see where this is leading? Don't they care? Here is one possibility.

Before we get too righteous about this issue, let's think about it from the point of view of someone who lives in a developing country. On one view, children are an asset. The more children I have, the more assets I have. My family is a work force that can help me to achieve what I want in life. They will do what I ask, even if I don't pay them very much. My children are not going to go on strike for better pay. When I retire, my children will look after me. No children, no retirement plan. Perhaps that's why I want children.

I should say here that there are other competing explanations. One may have intended to have fewer children, but that intent is frustrated by a lack of knowledge about birth control, a lack of access to contraceptives, or religious beliefs that impede it. One may have more children to compensate for a high rate of infant mortality.

Things are quite different in the first world for three reasons. First, the fact that machines do everything means that an oversized family workforce is likely to be more of a liability than an asset. Second, employed people in the first world usually have savings to fund their retirement. Third, infant mortality is very low in the first world.

As far as reasons to have a small family in the third world, they are weak. The overpopulation problem does not affect me very directly. If the grazing land, or the fishing stocks, or the potable water is running out, then my personal interest is best advanced by grabbing as much of it for myself as I can, not conserving it. This problem, which is frequently encountered in economics and life, is called the "Tragedy of the Commons" and also the "Prisoners' Dilemma."

The basic idea is that two people have a choice whether to cooperate or not. The payoffs are organised in such a way that if both people cooperate, then both will be better off. However, if one cooperates and the other does not, then the non-co-operator gets a big advantage, while the co-operator suffers a heavy penalty. If neither cooperates, then they each suffer a small penalty.

The two people cannot communicate. They must come to their separate conclusions about what to do. It so happens, given these payoffs, that the dominant strategy is not to cooperate. Moving from this hypothetical game situation to the real world, we can see a reason for the different outcomes in the first and third worlds.

Because of the way the Prisoner's Dilemma game works, the third world finds it hard to achieve the best outcome by co-operating.

Reduced access to education opportunities is one factor that works against the cooperative solution. In the first world, however, where people find it easier to communicate and to understand the rules of this game, it is easier to reach an agreement on cooperating to achieve the best outcome.

What economists say about this

What I just said might seem sensible to you, or perhaps not. There are certainly other possible explanations for what demographers see, such as cultural or religious beliefs, differences in access to birth control across countries and groups within countries, female education levels, and many other ideas. How do we make sense of all these conflicting explanations?

An economist named Gary Becker developed a parsimonious theory that can explain these fertility differences between different parts of the world. Parsimony means thrift, which is related to efficiency, so you can see why such a theory would appeal to economists. What is good about this theory is that you don't need to assume very much about parents' motivation to have children or their decision about how much money to spend on each child.

Rather than paraphrase Professor Becker and his colleagues, I will take the unusual step of quoting the abstract to one of their papers:[1]

> *Our analysis of growth assumes endogenous fertility and a rising rate of return on human capital as the stock of human capital increases. When human capital is abundant, rates of return on human capital investments are high relative to rates of return on children, whereas when human capital is scarce, rates of return on human capital are low relative to those on children. As a result, societies with limited human capital choose large families and invest little in each member; those with abundant human capital do the opposite. This leads to two stable steady states. One has large families and little human capital; the other has small families and perhaps growing human and physical capital.*

Here is an economist's explanation of what demographers see. The human capital they refer to is the knowledge a person gains through education and meaningful work experience. The return on this human capital is the higher wage that such an educated person earns because that person is a more productive worker. In order to obtain these high returns to knowledge and know-how, it is helpful to be working in an environment with a lot of different types of machines and complex organisations that require high level skills to operate or manage.

When Becker says that fertility is endogenous, what he means is that the model allows people to choose their own fertility—deciding how many children to have—based on a rational choice that takes account of their likely returns to each type of strategy.

What he found was that in an environment already rich in human capital (a well-educated, diverse workforce), people will choose to have fewer children and invest heavily in their education. However, in an environment poor in human capital, such as in a subsistence economy largely based on agriculture or primary production, people will choose to have many children, but not invest very much in their education.

To decide what to make of this analysis, note that this particular article has nearly 3,000 citations. That means that it has been referred to by 3,000 other scientific articles. It may not seem like a lot to someone with 100,000 facebook followers. However, each citation represents the fact that someone has read this 27 page article, and it influenced that second author's own research direction, culminating in another published, peer-reviewed article. Given those points, 3,000 citation is an impressive achievement. These citations establish the original article as a significant part of the blockchain of the science of economics.

Professor Becker is a Nobel prize winner in economics. That doesn't necessarily mean his theory is right. Nor does the high number of citations or even the parsimony of his approach. In fact it's hard to ever know if a particular theory is right. Nevertheless, it is an attractive theory because it matches the empirical work so far and it has an elegant, minimalist foundation in plausible assumptions. Best of all, it leads to testable predictions, it can help to build other theories to explain other important problems, and it suggests a way to resolve the population explosion in developing countries.

The emphasis in Becker's work is on the abundance of human capital in a society. That is the factor that determines whether parents choose to have many children and invest very little in each one, or to have few children but invest strongly in each one. Helping developing countries to develop more of that human capital would be a good step, for them and for us. Even if we look at these things from a narrow perspective of self-interest, providing the right help to the developing world will enhance our own survival prospects.

Of course, not everyone sees it this way. Let's explore that contrary viewpoint and evaluate how well it is faring as a basis for policy.

Containment breached

For a very long time, the third world's population explosion was not our problem. The huddled masses huddled in their own countries. They had a lot of trouble communicating their pain to people in the first world. At that time, they had no power to bring their problem to our doorstep. The borders were hard to cross. One might say that this problem was "contained."

Tough border controls were portrayed as tough love for these third world countries. They forced these countries to do something about their own population problems because no one else would help them. By rising to that challenge and solving their problems, these countries would be better off, eventually. Some countries, like China, went so far as to make rules that a family can only have one child. When it was in force, from 1979 to 2015, this rule led onlookers from countries that don't have severe demographic pressures (mainly in Western Europe) to suffer from ethical qualms. Despite that sense of disquiet, from a practical standpoint it actually worked in slowing down China's population growth.[2]

It is possible that those who police the borders don't care what happens to the countries across the fence. Being charitable, though, we might imagine the border authority as the captain of a submarine that's been hit by a torpedo. For the sake of the submarine, it is necessary to lock the bulkhead to contain the seawater. Unfortunately, the crew members who were in the flooded, now locked compartment will drown, but the price of getting them out is the sinking of the submarine and all aboard it.

Reasoning by metaphor, which is something else that economists like to do, has the problem that alternative metaphors can lead you in different directions. Instead of a submarine, perhaps it is the cruise ship Titanic. Instead of a torpedo launched by a hostile force, perhaps it's an iceberg that the captain encountered through incompetence. The decision to lock the steerage passengers in the bottom part of the sinking ship was not necessary to stop the ship from sinking. The ship would sink regardless.

The reason for the lock-in was that there weren't enough lifeboats for everyone aboard. It was a simple zero sum game. The border authority in this case didn't want steerage passengers displacing aristocrats from the scarce lifeboat seats. On this view, a tough borders policy is not grounded in a sense of the common good, but rather self-interest.

Whatever the interpretation, lately, this containment strategy is failing. Refugees are better organised and better at penetrating these borders. Isolated acts of violence become more common on the home soil of first world countries. These terror acts serve as a reminder that the suffering in third world countries is a problem for first world citizens, too.

Terror is shocking, as it is meant to be. Confronted with it, it is understandable that people react in emotional ways. Some of these reactions are not helpful to finding a solution, either for the first world inhabitants or the third world.

It is helpful to remember that a lot of people in developing countries would be content to stay there if there wasn't a war going on. There wouldn't be as many wars if the economies of these countries were performing better. They would perform better if restrictions on trade were relaxed. The conflicts that do occur would not be as devastating if the arms manufacturers in the developed world didn't provide so many weapons to every side in these disputes.

Let's think about what economics can tell us about this particular set of problems. Some policies of first world countries have external effects on third world countries. Protectionist trade policies in the first world countries make it harder for some third world countries to trade with them, entrenching the poverty trap that some of them experience. The sale of small arms manufactured in first world countries to actors in third world countries exacerbate and prolong some conflicts in those countries, leading to displaced civilian populations, pressures for emigration, and ill feeling toward some first world countries.

How does an affected country internalise this externality so that the parties who are causing the problem feel their pain, too? There are not many options, but any that involve rational dialogue have an obvious attractiveness compared to the alternatives.

3.2 Elegant sufficiency

We've been exploring one kind of limit to growth where, metaphorically speaking, the plant's roots have spread far enough to encounter the edge of the pot. In this chapter, I'd like to explore a different kind of limit. Some plants don't grow into hundred foot tall trees, even when they have the space and nutrients to do it. What if we lose the will to grow bigger? What if we decide we are satisfied? Is that something that could happen to the human race? Would we still be called a "race" if we stopped running?

There are unmistakeable signs that this is happening to us now. I will investigate how some of us are responding to this new situation. Then I will explain why a lack of desire for growth might happen in theory and consider what the evidence says about it.

Not enough death now

No one ever imagined that people would run out of dead things to burn, but we are approaching that point now. People have become so successful at surviving that our population is out of control. The species that poses the most wide-spread and gravest threat to the sustainability of life on earth is us. You see, growth used to be a solution to our main problem, but now it has become our main problem. It's a bit like cane toads.

Growth requires raw materials, and there are so many of us now that there isn't enough of that material on the whole planet. The earth is round, which means that it is finite. This represents one type of limit to growth. Let's call this the supply of growth potential. It's running out, and even the dumbest politician in the world can see that.

There is another type of limit to growth that isn't much talked about, but I think we should look into it. Let's call this the demand for growth potential. This is also petering out, and even the smartest politicians in the world are denying it.

We have seen that growth is important, and that it has mostly been driven by population growth to date. What are the prospects for growth when the population is steady? Not as bountiful as you might expect. A lot of the growth that seems to be happening is like cancer—it makes us sicker. Here are some examples.

An astroturf arms race

The second amendment to the constitution of the United States contains some ambiguous words that were written at a time when an irregular army, or militia, succeeded in defeating the British Army to win the independence of which Americans are so proud. These words are interpreted to mean that Americans have a right to own guns of any type they like. There are a lot of guns in America, and gun violence is very common. It would be safer for all concerned if there were not so many guns and if there was no right to own them in the constitution.

During the Cold War, America and Russia had a competition to see who could build the most and strongest atomic bombs. This arms race went on for a long time. By the time sense prevailed, each side had enough firepower to destroy the entire planet several times over. Since then, disarmament treaties have been negotiated. There are still atom bombs, but now the destructive power is smaller. Both sides worked out that they only needed to be able to destroy Earth once each.

The thing about an arms race is that it is very difficult to stop once you've started. You want to stop, because you understand how risky it is and how much it costs to keep going, but you can't stop. It is another form of the Prisoner's Dilemma game I mentioned before. Whatever the other contestant does, your own best move is to build more arms.

This is part of the explanation for the gun problem in America. You would prefer everyone to be disarmed, but whether they are or not, *you* would feel safer if you had a gun yourself. About 40% of American households look at it this way. This means that the 'militia' that is mentioned in the second amendment is ready to overthrow the government, if necessary.

Another feature of an arms race is that it takes a long time for sense to prevail. In this case, people are slow to understand that a bunch of unhappy voters with pistols will not overthrow the US government, which has atomic bombs, an air force, a navy, and ways of knowing what treasonous malcontents are doing most of the time.[3]

Arms races are one way that growth can continue even when people don't want or need more products. Like many of these new growth 'opportunities,' it is built on a nonsensical proposition and is likely to do great harm in the longer run.

Addicted to addiction

One sure fire way to continue on a growth path is to become addicted to drugs, or gambling. There are some types of drugs that will make you grow into a bigger or stronger person, but that is not the sort of growth I am talking about. Growth in the number, type and value of products that are bought and sold is the topic of interest. Addiction is very helpful to this type of growth. It is helpful because it clouds your mind. It changes your perception of what you need.

Some addictions simply make you waste money buying things that don't help you to live a better life. These are fairly benign. Other addictions put your health at risk, and others make you take crazy risks to get the money you need to continue with the addiction. These are dangerous to you and to others.

It may seem strange, but the science of economics has great difficulty with the fact that addiction alters your sense of priorities. It is normal for economic scientists to begin every task with the assumptions that people know what they want and that they should be free to have it if they can afford to. Economists have normally rejected any attempt by moralisers to tell other people what they should want.

While there are good reasons for that attitude, it becomes a problem when what people want is to inject heroin or play Russian Roulette. Here is the problem: our present theory of economics has no principle that would allow someone to say that these preferences are different than a preference to eat a wholesome meal when hungry.

Applying one test of reasonableness—what would a six year old think?—if our theory of economics refuses to say that a lethal form of entertainment is a bad choice, then perhaps that theory of economics needs to be re-examined.

The fountain of youth

Some people enjoy life so much that they want it to go on forever, but this is easier said than done. As people get older, more things go wrong with their bodies. Fixing these problems gets more complicated and expensive in old age. We have seen, in the 20th century, that it is possible to spend a huge amount of money trying to live longer. Here is a possible way to keep the economy growing in size and value, even though the population isn't.

Over a long period of time, the average life expectancy of humans has increased. There are four main reasons for this: less warfare, good plumbing, more food, and better science. In the first world, the first two reasons have gone about as far as they can go. The last reason, better science, can go further. However, offsetting that, the third reason has gone too far. People are eating more than is healthy for them. Because of this, for the first time in more than 100 years, average life expectancy is going back down. As individuals, we are spending more on health. Governments are spending more on health, and people are living shorter lives.

Once again, we are seeing something that looks like growth, but it is an illusion. Economic activity—buying and selling—is going faster, and the dollar values are getting bigger. Much of this per capita growth, though, is part of some arms race, an addiction, or a fruitless quest to live longer. We seem to be growing because we are wandering, faster and faster, more furiously than ever before, but getting nowhere. We don't know what we want.

Motivation and personality

The psychologist Abraham Maslow developed a theory of motivation and personality that he described in a book of that name. Famously, he set out a set of basic human needs that formed a pyramid structure—a hierarchy of needs. Nowadays, management theorists all have their own versions of this approach, and many practitioners pour cold water on the empirical foundations of that book. However, Maslow's original idea is very durable. It has captured the public imagination. Without claiming to know anything much about psychology, I adopt Maslow's need hierarchy in order to explore the question of what will make us keep working after we've had enough to eat. I will use slightly different language to Maslow. I hope this won't misrepresent his intentions.

There are five layers in the hierarchy. According to the theory, a person will focus exclusively on attaining satisfaction at the present layer before contemplating moving to the next layer up the pyramid.

The lowest and most basic need is for oxygen, water, food, and sleep. Borrowing a term from biology, these are the things an organism needs to achieve homoeostasis. If starving, thirsty or sleep deprived, a person will think of nothing else until that problem is overcome.

Once homoeostatic, a person's next type of need is for safety. Safety requires shelter, such as a house or apartment, and an environment where threats from wild animals, thuggish people and disease are controlled. A well-fed but insecure person will think of nothing else until he is safe.

A safe, homoeostatic person's next type of need is for love and belongingness, which usually comes from spending time with friends and family. At this layer, the hierarchy idea becomes a bit less strict. It is probably not accurate to say that a safe person thinks of nothing but love and belongingness until satisfied on that issue. Relationships are complicated. One has to hold down a job and progress in a career while waiting for the perfect partner, or despite breaking up with one.

Having achieved a reasonably acceptable level of love and belongingness, a person's next type of need is for esteem and self-esteem. This is mainly about the feelings toward you that are held by people who are not necessarily your friends or lovers. It has a lot to do with your position in society, your profession, and your professional accomplishments.

Maslow mentioned a fifth layer, which is self-actualisation. I don't pretend to understand that very well. In any case, it is not so important for the economic analysis of growth prospects that I'd now like to launch into.

How the economy meets Maslow's needs

The economy can help people to achieve homoeostasis efficiently by mass-producing food. A primitive society can grow its economy by producing food more efficiently. This form of growth is limited, though, by the fact that people will normally stop buying more food when they're not hungry any more. Some ingenious tricks can be used to make people pay more money for every calorie, or to overeat, but at the end of the day, a calorie is a calorie and people only need so many a week to be healthy.

It may amaze you to learn that this is the full extent to which industrial output for private consumption can be used to directly satisfy human needs—that is, if Maslow's theory is correct. The higher level needs cannot be directly satisfied by buying more stuff.

For example, the safety need can be met most effectively through collective action across all of society. Law and order is provided by the Government, not by a supermarket. Freedom from disease is provided largely through prevention—the eradication of dangerous germs and their vectors, vaccination, and universal public hygiene—none of which is possible without collective action. In short, consumers don't buy safety. Rather governments provide it and taxation makes it possible to do so.

People have an intuitive sense of how safe is safe enough. This varies between individuals, but everyone has a comfort zone. When you feel safe enough, you won't keep demanding that the Government does more. The economy can't keep growing forever by making people safer and safer.

Having said that, it is true that spending on safety will grow when threats are growing. That's how an arms race can supercharge growth. As we saw, though, this type of growth is not very practical or useful.

The need for love and belongingness, like the need for safety, cannot be met directly by purchasing something. The satisfiers of this need are your friends and family. To have a more satisfactory experience, you need to spend time with them. This provides a connection to the economy, but it is a more subtle one than a simple act of consumption. Your leisure time, which is the time you have to spend with friends and family, is the time that you don't have to be at work. Your job defines your leisure time in a negative way. Your partner's work schedule also defines your ability to use your own leisure time to improve the satisfaction that you both get.

There are some other connections to the economy. Social media provide a search capability that can help you to find someone you might like. It also helps to bridge the gap when travel and incompatible schedules make face-to-face time harder to get.

Given all these points, it is hard to see how the need for love and belongingness can drive any meaningful expansion in the economy. This type of satisfaction is something that happens while industry is making other plans.

The need for esteem and self-esteem, like the safety and love needs, cannot be satisfied by consumption. Certainly, esteem is a big topic. The elements of an estimable life are complicated and varied. However, we can say in general that people compete for estimable positions in society and these are often closely associated with the jobs or careers people have.

Right away we can see a connection to the economy, but not the sort of connection you might have expected. The things you do in pursuit of esteem, such as getting a university education or training to be an elite athlete, competing with other ambitious people for scarce spots at the apex of the pyramid all affect the economy. They affect the character and qualities of the economy, rather than its overall size and level of output.

The pursuit of esteem does not contribute very much to the growth of the economy. The fundamental problem is that coveted positions in society are scarce. Intentionally so. By design, these social limits to growth preclude significant expansion.

This, in a nutshell, explains why the sort of real per-capita growth that we became accustomed to in the 20th century is unlikely to keep going. Of course, it's just a theory. It's a theory of economics built on top of a theory of psychology from a famous psychologist who probably had no idea that his theory might be used in this way. What do the empirics say?

Real per capita growth is stalling

It is not very easy to directly confirm whether these ideas borrowed from Maslow have the implications for growth that I claim they do. However, I can point to two strands of empirical work that support that view. The first is a series of studies of what people buy when their income increases. This evidence supports the idea of a hierarchy of needs. The second is an examination of the movements in real per capita growth in the United States from 1750 to about 2007 (before the GFC).

Professor Engel first noticed that families spend a smaller fraction of their income on food as they have more money to spend. Since then, many other economists have documented the same phenomenon, also with clothing. The spending on some other types of services shows an opposite trend. In particular, travel, education and medical services. These facts, widely observed across different countries and different periods of time, are consistent with the idea that food and clothing serve lower level needs and that travel and education serve higher level needs, which can only be seriously entertained once the basic needs have been met.

Professor Robert Gordon, in a much-cited NBER article entitled, "Is U.S. Economic Growth Over? Faltering Innovation Confronts the Six Headwinds" documented and offered some possible explanations for stalling real per capita growth. His abstract noted,

> *This paper raises basic questions about the process of economic growth. It questions the assumption, nearly universal since Solow's seminal contributions of the 1950s, that economic growth is a continuous process that will persist forever. There was virtually no growth before 1750, and thus there is no guarantee that growth will continue indefinitely. Rather, the paper suggests that the rapid progress made over the past 250 years could well turn out to be a unique episode in human history. ...Growth in this frontier gradually accelerated after 1750, reached a peak in the middle of the 20th century, and has been slowing down since. The paper is about "how much further could the frontier growth rate decline?"*

> *The analysis links periods of slow and rapid growth to the timing of the three industrial revolutions (IR's), that is, IR #1 (steam, railroads) from 1750 to 1830; IR #2 (electricity, internal combustion engine, running water, indoor toilets, communications, entertainment, chemicals, petroleum) from 1870 to 1900; and*

IR #3 (computers, the web, mobile phones) from 1960 to present. It provides evidence that IR #2 was more important than the others and was largely responsible for 80 years of relatively rapid productivity growth between 1890 and 1972. Once the spin-off inventions from IR #2 (airplanes, air conditioning, interstate highways) had run their course, productivity growth during 1972-96 was much slower than before. In contrast, IR #3 created only a short-lived growth revival between 1996 and 2004. Many of the original and spin-off inventions of IR #2 could happen only once – urbanization, transportation speed, the freedom of females from the drudgery of carrying tons of water per year, and the role of central heating and air conditioning in achieving a year-round constant temperature.

Even if innovation were to continue into the future at the rate of the two decades before 2007, the U.S. faces six headwinds that are in the process of dragging long-term growth to half or less of the 1.9 percent annual rate experienced between 1860 and 2007. These include demography, education, inequality, globalization, energy/ environment, and the overhang of consumer and government debt. A provocative "exercise in subtraction" suggests that future growth in consumption per capita for the bottom 99 percent of the income distribution could fall below 0.5 percent per year for an extended period of decades.

The idea that growth might not continue is uncomfortable. Professor Gordon's reasoning is not the same as mine. His explanation is more about problems with the supply side than the demand side, which I am emphasising. Yet we are both focusing on the disappearance of opportunities for per capita growth.

Clearly, though, we may all need to get used to the idea of a lower rate of growth. We may also need to take a hard look at the aspects of life and community that depend on continuous growth. If we are vulnerable there, we may need time to prepare for a different course of action.

What have we misunderstood? Many of us harbour a naïve optimism that growth is good, that growth is inevitable and everlasting, and that growth will solve a lot of our problems. I hope to have shown you in this chapter that growth can be good in the right circumstances, but not in the circumstances that face us now. The other two propositions are false, representing an unrealistic hope.

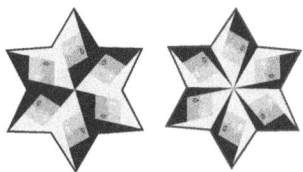

PART 2

MISUNDERSTANDING THE PRESENT

4

BULLETINS FROM A PANDEMIC

Even before the pandemic struck, the world was not in a happy place, as the foregoing chapters explain. Things veered from vexing to alarming in around March 2020 in my country. The trouble started earlier in places North of here. A lot of commentary focused on the damage that lockdowns were doing to the economy. Some economists even said we should bite the bullet, invite widespread infections and hope for herd immunity in a few months. Clearly, these economists knew nothing about epidemiology. Their cavalier attitude to important constraints on hospital capacity, personal protective equipment, ventilators and even oxygen tanks reflected poorly on their profession.

When I made the notes that you are about to read, I was trying to look beyond the immediate effects of the crisis and see what it was telling us about the way we might live in the future, what would return to normal one day and what would change permanently.

4.1 What COVID-19 will change forever

6 April 2020

The present pandemic is changing almost everything for almost everyone in the world. I'd like to try to imagine a future where the pandemic is over, people, societies, economies and countries have made the necessary adjustments, and most things return to normal. What are the things that won't return to normal?

I think, once a vaccine is developed and/or widespread immunity has been developed the hard way, people will return to socialising in person. Restaurants and bars, live performances of music and theatre, stadium sports and crowded beaches will all make a comeback. Despite the doomsayers, globalisation will creep back after a while. Supply chains will keep more inventory than before and will be less dependent on a single point of failure. But international trade won't go away. The efficiencies are just too compelling.

There is, however, a particular type of inefficiency that will disappear forever as a result of this pandemic. This inefficiency is caused by the need to do certain things in person in the company of others. The reason it hasn't been economised out of the system before is that the efficient alternatives are what is called "experience goods." Peoples' lack of familiarity with these alternatives were a barrier to take-up. People were reluctant to take the first step and try them.

The pandemic has forced people, in lockdown or other forms of temporary isolation, to take that first step. People are experiencing these alternatives, finding out how to make them work, and discovering that the experience, while not the same as the 'real thing', is not actually all that bad. Because of the immense savings of time and money from doing things in this new remote tele-working way, I predict that people will never go back, even when they have the option to do so.

What are these certain things that people have done inefficiently for so long? The so-called "bricks and mortar" retail sector is one example. It was in trouble before the pandemic because an online shopping experience was so much cheaper and the range of products available was incomparably superior. No one will *go* shopping any more. They will shop without going anywhere. COVID-19 will be the last nail in that coffin.

Going to university will be replaced by logging on to university. A large proportion of a university student's experience will happen remotely. If this comes to pass, as looks very likely now, the ramifications will be enormous. Countries like Australia will lose a lot of overseas students and with them a lot of export income. These foreign students will go to Harvard or Oxford, instead, or one of the other top 100 world universities. You might think that most of them won't get accepted there, but you would be wrong. These elite universities will be able to expand their capacity once they don't have to physically accommodate their students.

Going to the doctor will be largely replaced by tele-health. General practitioners will be able to use their time better, see more patients each day, and not make the patients suffer the risk of cross-infections in the waiting room. A specialist will be able to analyse your scans from a distant office and provide advice that is just as good as the advice you would get in person. Once robotic surgery gets a bit better, there will be no need for the surgeon to be in the same operating theatre as the patient, or even the same country. The medical profession is being forced to do some of this now, and by doing they will get very proficient at it.

More profoundly, going to work will become a totally different experience for people in all the professions and anyone involved in knowledge work. I don't think that people will keep doing business meetings by skype from their bedrooms after the pandemic. Full time work from home will probably not be feasible for psychological reasons as much as anything else.

What will happen, though, is that people will find they don't need to come into the office every day even when working full time. They won't need to commute at peak hour. Their employers won't need such large offices. The public transport networks, which are sized to handle peak crowds, will be able to be smaller and run more efficiently—they won't need as many trains or buses. City car parks won't need to be as big.

Real estate prices will change drastically. Commercial real estate will suffer a triple whammy from smaller offices, fewer retail outlets and smaller educational land requirements. Workers, who will be less tightly bound to their places of work, will be able to reside further away. They might prefer the ambience of the coast, the mountains or even farming districts. In short, people won't need to live in the cities in order to do their jobs so they will spread out.

Amenity and cost will push them away from crowded places, and the residential land price gradient will flatten out. There could even be a resurgence of country towns as knowledge workers move there and keep their city jobs. Their city salaries would help them to live a pretty nice lifestyle in those towns, and the boost in local income would help to turn things around for places that have lost population to the coastal megacities for a hundred years.

These predictions might sound crazy to someone who doesn't want to let go of the life, society and economy we had as recently as two months ago. But something profound has changed in that time. We have been forced to try remote working. We were reluctant to take that step, but now that we have, I suspect there will be no going back to the shops, to university, to the doctor or even to work as we knew it. There will be winners and losers, but the new way will be a lot less wasteful of time and resources. People will have more choice about where they live and more jobs to choose from.

4.2 Irrational behaviour even a President could understand

22 March 2020

What do toilet paper hoarding, ticket scalping and empty dams have in common? They are each examples of what economists call the inventory problem. The first two are non-problems that people get irrationally worked up about. The third thing is a calculated risk that we take when we trade-off security of supply for cost-savings. That trade-off is a bigger gamble in these uncertain times.

Inventory, as any merchant knows, is stuff that you keep in storage so that you can sell it, use it to make something, or simply consume it later on. It represents a safety buffer. If deliveries get messed up, it lets you carry on selling, making or consuming until they get back to normal. You often think of manufacturing businesses that need raw materials and spare parts, or canned goods on supermarket shelves, but drinking water in dams and reservoirs is also an example of a kind of inventory. Our recent experiences with drought highlight the importance of the security we get from having full water storages.

The thing that most people don't understand is that keeping inventory is costly. The more you have on hand, the greater the cost. The longer you have to store it for, the greater the cost. The simplest way to think of this cost is to imagine that you have to borrow money to buy inventory and you only pay the loan back when the inventory is sold or used. The holding cost is related, in fact, to interest rates. So, you want to minimise your holding cost by holding less, although when interest rates are low you might choose to hold a bit more.

Trouble is that when you save money by reducing inventory, you increase the risk that you will run out of something you need. Especially when the supply chains are disrupted by some unforeseen event like, say, a global pandemic of a highly infectious and deadly disease.

"Just-In-Time" (JIT) supply chain arrangements minimise the amount of inventory needed at every step in the supply chain. A carburettor arrives just in time to build the car engine, and then that engine along with the wheels, brakes and windscreen arrive just in time to build the car. Minimum inventory sitting around means minimum holding costs. This all works fine, as long as the ballet of the logistics chain follows the musical score.

All supermarket chains and most manufacturing companies use JIT because it represented the best trade-off between cost and risk that some very smart people chose a few years ago. At that time, when the JIT logistics revolution was flavour of the month, risks of disruption seemed low. It was full steam ahead with cost reduction.

Now that so much of the world is in social and economic lockdown, it is timely to re-evaluate that trade-off and perhaps rebalance in favour of a bit more cost for more secure supply. I have no doubt that the global logistics empires will work something out, and that is certainly comforting as we have become very reliant on them.

But there is also an inventory problem at the household level, and here I am not so confident that everything will work out quickly. For the most part, we have our own pantries and freezers. We've worked out how often we need to shop and expect that we'll find what we need when we go shopping. Only now, with a viral apocalypse at the doorstep, our supermarket visits make us think we're in Cold War East Berlin. Unbelievably, fights are breaking out in the aisles over toilet paper. The police are called to stop it.

I said earlier that this was a non-problem, but I may need to clarify that thought. Getting punched in the face at the supermarket is certainly a problem. However, the lack of supplies at the supermarket is a non-problem (if you can wait a bit) because there has been no disruption to the source of supply. Crops are still being planted, harvested and packaged. Toilet paper continues to grow on trees. All the groceries are at the distribution centre and will get to the store soon enough, if people would just calm down.

Politicians could also help themselves to be more effective. Here are a few simple measures that they could take: (1) answer the questions you are asked by the press, and (2) tell the truth. If they could establish a reputation for straight talking, then when they tell people that they will be all right if they stop panicking, people would stop panicking. This would be a refreshing change in attitude all around.

Let's talk about a different type of inventory: cash or money in the bank. Some people were low on this type of inventory even before things turned sour. These people don't have any way of increasing their personal inventory by paying higher prices. They're nearly broke, and major disruption can push them over the edge. As some wag in the press put it recently, it isn't the poor and indigent who are buying pallet loads of toilet paper from Costco.

So we come now to profiteering. I also said this was a non-problem, and I'm willing to cop some heat for sticking with that opinion. When things don't go your way, it is always tempting and sometimes comforting to blame it on hoarders, super-spreaders, people smugglers, ticket scalpers, congressional democrats, senate republicans, or any other group the cut of whose jib you don't like. Let's think about this like economists, and with particular focus on the inventory problem.

On Monday, I go to a supermarket in an out-of-the-way place where they haven't put restrictions in yet, and buy all the tinned corn in the store. I take it all down to the self-storage unit I rented for the purpose and wait for the price of tinned corn in Blackheath to go through the roof. Then I will clean up. Unfortunately, my attempt to corner the market will fail. There's lots more tinned corn where that came from. The price won't move at all. It will take me decades to eat it all. I should have picked something I like.

So, normal market forces will prevent anyone making money from a temporary glitch in the supply chain. What about ticket scalping? At least there it is actually possible to corner the market for a Bob Dylan concert on a particular date, if you've got enough money. Here again, the basic story is an inventory problem. Under normal market conditions, scalping should not be profitable.

Let's say that the Dylan tickets are valued on average at $100 by members of the public. If I buy all the tickets at $100 each, I can expect to make no cash profit by reselling them. Worse, I had to borrow $1m to buy the 10,000 tickets, so I'm looking at a hefty interest bill. I'm going to lose money.

In order to make money, I'd have to buy the tickets for, say $80 each. But if they're valued by customers at $100, why would the concert organisers sell them for less than that? Here is one possible reason. It is important for marketing (of both the venue and the artist) to be able to say that a concert was sold out. The only way I can be sure of selling out is to under-price the tickets. When you look at it in this way, all that is happening is that the scalpers get some of the profit that the concert organisers might otherwise have gotten. People pay their valuation for the tickets either way. If anyone has been disadvantaged, it is the concert organiser, but that was a decision the organiser took on rational grounds, so we should not feel sympathetic. In short, scalping is a non-problem.

Rather than waste too much time agonising over non-problems, or doubting the profit-maximising skills of commercial enterprises that are big enough to take care of themselves, we would be well served by focusing on the real problems. In this episode, the real problems I've highlighted are trust, civility, and ignorance of economics. Let's get them right and then a lot of these other things that trouble us so much will sort themselves out.

4.3 POTUS misunderstands economic impact of COVID19

13 March 2020

A President recently banned travellers from Europe entering his country. In explaining why this was no big deal for the economy, he had this to say on twitter:

> *Hoping to get the payroll tax cut approved by both Republicans and Democrats, and please remember, very important for all countries & businesses to know that* trade will in no way be affected by the 30-day restriction on travel from Europe. The restriction stops people not goods.

121K 1:13 PM – Mar 12, 2020

Taking a contrarian position to the 121,000 people who liked that pronouncement, the stockmarket had this to say:

> *Wall Street suffers another trading halt as coronavirus crisis and Trump travel ban cause shares to plunge*
>
> **https://www.abc.net.au/news/2020-03-13/wall-street-halts-trade-financial-markets-coronavirus/12051742**

One is bound to ask, where is the cognitive failure?

It is certainly true that the stock market can overreact to news, both bad and good. If it is a mirror of the economy, it is one of those distorting funhouse mirrors that makes you look fat when you aren't.

The distortion occurs because the stock market is a place where investors bet on the future—they speculate on where each titbit of new information might propel other investors. It is always tricky second-guessing the herd. More so when it is a herd of second-guessers.

Meanwhile, in the real economy (where real news motivates real people to do things that matter) COVID19 quarantine rules are clearly hurting tourism, airlines, education, and live entertainment including sport. Economists can measure the size of these industries and estimate the effect of, say, a 25% drop off in these forms of trade.

The secondary effects are much more difficult to measure in normal times. That is because economists are usually unable to perform experiments with the economy. Imagine getting that past the ethics committee! One (admittedly small) silver lining is that this episode of global economic contraction presents a fascinating opportunity to study and quantify these secondary effects.

Back to the problem with that tweet, my Italian shoes or my Skoda can still be delivered, but I may have to meet my German business colleague by skype because she is banned from Boston. If she is trying to sell me something, I may decide not to buy it because I couldn't speak to her in person. I can still ship my Chevy to Kiev, but the Ukrainian market may have gone cold on US exports.

More generally, while trade in goods may not be cruelled by a travel ban on people, trade in services will be. What we're talking about is not just haircuts and weight loss programs. Services include a lot of valuable stuff like tourism, transport, legal, accounting, engineering and even economic advice. How important is trade in services? According to the Reserve Bank of Australia, services accounted for more than 23% of the value of global trade in 2017, up from 17% in 1980.

https://www.rba.gov.au/publications/bulletin/2019/mar/ the-international-trade-in-services.html

So, even allowing for the tendency of the stockmarket to catastrophise, that President made a mistake. He didn't understand the importance of services to the world, and even to his own economy.

4.4 Who will rescue the capitalists?

14 April 2020

Like many of you, I have been wondering how best to understand the economic impact of the COVID-19 pandemic. In the counterfactual world: if governments had let the virus have its way, there would certainly be more businesses operating than today, but it would not be business as usual. More workers would miss work because they are sick. A lot of people would avoid crowds even if the government didn't make them. If we assumed that the fatality rate of the disease stayed within the currently observed non-crisis range of around 1% to 4%, the death toll would be appalling, but the human race would survive.

Of course, in this laissez-faire world there is a strong possibility of a complete breakdown of public health systems. Once that happened, you could take that fatality rate and multiply it by a significant number. It wouldn't just be COVID-19 infectees dying of preventable causes, but also people who need to go to hospital for other reasons and who would normally expect to recover. We would start to see a significant effect on the world population, but not extinction of our species. None of that speculation takes account of the possibility that in a rampant pandemic the virus might mutate into more deadly, more infectious and even less treatable forms.

Governments have been mostly convinced by this that do-nothing was not a viable policy. So we have closed borders and closed certain workplaces to contain the spread of infections. To understand how these steps affect the economy, we need to look at the types of workplaces that have been closed. There are two main types of businesses:

1. Long distance travel, because that travel itself is a disease vector
2. Activities involving uncontrollable human contact.

In more relaxed times, we often classify businesses according to their capital intensity (robotic car factories at one end and dog walkers at the other), but classifying businesses according to their potential for human contact is something new. Looking at workplaces through this lens, there are three types of interactions to consider:

- Staff to staff
- Customer to staff
- Customer to customer

Where staff are concerned, it is usually feasible for the manager to arrange things so that staff are unlikely to infect each other. Staff members do predictable things in pre-planned ways, and can be expected to follow company policies about distancing and protective clothing.

Where customers are concerned, face-to-face contact is much more difficult to control. Sports stadiums, live entertainment, pubs and eat-in restaurants have all been closed for this reason. Note that almost all of these businesses provide discretionary, rather than essential services.

The people who work in businesses forced to close now get government wage support in Australia (the JobKeeper payments). This helps to avoid an amplified demand shock that could make things in the economy a lot worse.

But businesses employ capital as well as labour. While it's nice to have a degree of protection for the providers of labour, what will happen to the providers of capital in the pandemic? To answer that, we need to drill a bit deeper. Does the business proprietor own the asset or rent it from someone else? Did the owner borrow money to buy the asset? If the business proprietor doesn't have any income mid-pandemic, what will happen to the asset if there's no money to pay the rent? How will the asset owner pay the interest on the debt used to buy it?

In normal times, a renter that doesn't pay the rent on time can get evicted, and a borrower that doesn't pay the interest on time may find that the bank takes possession of the asset. The landlord just finds someone else to rent the property. The bank just sells the asset to someone else. In a worst case, owners of capital might just take their money to a different country where prospects are better.

But, as I don't need to tell you, these are not normal times. With our country in lockdown, there is no one else who will lease a vacant restaurant or concert hall from the landlord. There is no one else to buy the foreclosed asset from the bank. In this global epidemic, there is no other country with better prospects for the capital owner. So, the renter's problem is also the landlord's problem. The borrower's problem is also the bank's problem.

How this plays out in any individual case depends on the fine print in the contracts and, if push comes to shove, on who has the better bargaining position—meaning a more attractive set of alternatives. One thing that the contract writers probably didn't anticipate was a worldwide epidemic of a highly contagious and potentially deadly disease that would double unemployment and close a wide range of industries virtually overnight. When the contracts are incomplete—meaning that they don't cover the situation we're in now—bargaining position becomes especially important.

Governments are grappling with the problems of rent and interest relief right now. They are not easy problems because so much depends on the particular circumstances of each case. A prudent government doesn't want to make a general rule that won't fit a majority of cases. The announced policies so far appear to amount to a request that parties act reasonably: that landlords and lenders treat their delinquent customers leniently if those customers are trying their hardest. In other words, it's a request that parties do what they are forced by economic necessity to do anyway, lacking feasible alternatives. It is making a virtue of a necessity.

Some assets are strategic. It is not in the public interest that these assets be sold by distressed owners at fire sale prices. The Commonwealth has already anticipated this particular failure mode and moved to tighten up the foreign investment rules to prevent it.

Passenger aircraft are certainly in that strategic category, although we may not need as many as we now have for the next few decades. If you have Boeing shares, you probably missed your chance to exit gracefully unless you did so in February. Government support for the airline industry makes sense in concept, although certainly not at any price.

Cruise ships are probably not in the strategic category. It is not hard to foresee a lean time for the cruising industry and an even leaner time for passenger shipbuilding. As for the existing ocean liners, there may be an opportunity to repurpose them as floating hospitals, fully equipped with ventilators, MRI machines and all that jazz, that could provide relief capacity to (coastal) cities in need.

So, where does all this speculation leave us? Government decisions to close down particular types of businesses mean that the services provided by those businesses are no longer available. For the most part, these represent discretionary purchases rather than essential services.

The employees of these businesses, who are numerous because the businesses mostly tend to be labour-intensive, are receiving a reasonably good level of government support. This prevents a multiplier effect from causing leveraged damage to the economy. The cost of that support is increased government debt, but no one who experienced the 1930s would question its necessity.

The owners of the assets that make the economy go, including land, machinery and even loans, will have to accept a reduced or zero return on their investment for a time. They will try to shift that burden as much as they can, but as we noted earlier, these capitalists can't choose from a rich menu of alternatives. If it is any consolation to them, at least machines will not depreciate very quickly if they're not being used. Obsolescence won't be a huge problem, either. There won't be much spending on R&D to improve the performance of idle machines. The opportunity cost of capital is and will remain low for a while. The smart money is in cash, earning a return of zero.

One reads a lot of inflammatory analysis that asks how much GDP we should trade for the human lives that will be lost to an unchecked COVID-19 epidemic. Most of that analysis assumes that letting the epidemic run riot will result in an economy that looks like the economy we had in December 2019. It also assumes that the medically safe version of the economy will see everybody ruined.

On the contrary, I hope to have persuaded you to look at a hibernation as possibly the best option for the economy as well as public health, in a version of the longer term in which we are not all dead!

4.5 Which furniture must we save from the inferno?

25 May 2020

A minority of economists say that Australia, New Zealand and other COVID containment strategy nations have dug ourselves into a hole by putting the economy into the deep freeze with no timeline on an exit strategy.

It is obviously too early to say whether the herd immunity strategy economies will perform any better in the medium term. One thing is clear, though. They will fare worse if they belatedly find they must switch to a containment strategy once the virus is ubiquitous.

Those economists in the minority have emphasised an age-related divide between those most vulnerable to the disease (the elderly) and those most vulnerable to the economic consequences of measures to contain it (the young). They say that policy has erred in favouring the elderly who are said to impose a net burden on the economy, even in normal times.

Let's leave aside the point that economists are not qualified to make sweeping judgements on medical policy or to predict the possible biological trajectory of an uncontrolled pandemic. That would be like giving a Lepidopterist veto power over the Reserve Bank Board's interest rate decisions. An uncontrolled pandemic could morph into something more dangerous in ways that economists are unlikely to predict. Economists' predictive skills are unimpressive even within their own field.

Let's also leave aside the breathtaking value judgements implicit in a policy almost designed to sacrifice the old for the good of the young. Economists are most comfortable, and others most comfortable with them, when they provide a value-neutral decision framework and let others decide their own preferences in a market or democratic setting. Few would be happy to accept an economist's advice on who should live and who should die.

Instead of dwelling on these valid criticisms, let us consider how we can best prepare the economy for the reboot. For this task, a medical metaphor seems apt. We can triage economic inputs to help us focus our efforts on those ones where intervention will make the greatest difference to our eventual success.

First, there are those inputs that will survive (or regenerate) even if we don't do anything. Many labour-intensive industries where workers do not have highly specific skills were hard hit by the lockdown because these industries feature a lot of face-to-face interaction which had to cease. Hospitality and tourism come to mind as possible examples. However, these same industries will suffer relatively little asset destruction as a result of the lockdown because they are not asset-intensive. Beyond payments to get unemployed people through the hibernation period, government support for these industries would not provide strategic benefit to the economy.

Second, there are those inputs that will be permanently transformed by the pandemic whatever we do. Some of these industries, such as bricks and mortar retail, in-person tertiary education, and commercial office space, were teetering on the brink of obsolescence (or at least radical shrinkage) even before the pandemic. The necessity of shopping, studying and working from home during the lockdown has shown us all how easy it is to adopt more efficient ways of doing things. It is hard to see these industries going back to normal after the pandemic, with or without government support.

Third, there are those inputs that are very hard to replace once they are damaged, compromised or destroyed by the current emergency—the furniture that we need to save from the fire. This is where government support would create strategic benefits. Which economic inputs are in this category?

It is natural to think of physical assets like factories, aircraft, and supercomputers. These are certainly assets that are very important to a modern economy. However, some of them (power stations and water treatment plants) have remained in operation throughout this crisis. Others, like aircraft, will come out of mothballs pretty much as they went in. Missing several months of wear and tear will not reduce their useful lives. Even the risk of being superseded by some newer technology is reduced in a viral pandemic—who will prioritise research to develop better machines to do a job that doesn't need to be done?

The critical assets are intellectual capital—the particular skills and knowhow of educated, experienced people. Specialisation in the economy amplifies the value of these people by allowing them to focus on the tasks they are uniquely suited to do. The dependence is mutual. These specialists can only function highly when they are in particular types of roles. The particular company needs them and they need the particular company. A nuclear physicist could get a job at Target, but her training would be wasted there.

Here is one important example of strategic government support. A program like the Australian Government's JobKeeper program helps to keep skilled workers connected with their skill-requiring jobs while the downturn affects the business. By doing this, it helps to avoid the destruction of relationship capital—knowhow—that is so important to a well-functioning economy.

Now we can return to the starting point of this article—the minority view among some economists that the economy would be best served by unrestrained human contact and the risk of mass contagion that entails. If human intellectual capital is important, then we must recognise that this capital is held to a large degree by older people, who have lived long enough to develop relevant experience. These people have spent decades solving hard problems, so they often know what works and what doesn't.

Reporting of the epidemic has focused attention on cruise ships and nursing homes where, presumably, the affected people were not actively engaged in the supply side of the economy. The fact that mass outbreaks in Australia have largely been confined to these types of venues is a sign of the success of our containment efforts.

However, a strategy of letting the virus run free would pose a serious threat to the older people who hold so much of society's knowledge and experience. Not just retirees, but also people who bring unique skills to difficult and important jobs now. People on whom our economy's future success depends. Let's not be too quick to feed the fire with this furniture.

Declaration of interest: the author is aged over 60 and employed.

5

BULLETINS FROM AN INSURRECTION

The other big news from 2020 was the train wreck that ended the Trump administration. This was certainly not disconnected from the pandemic, but really it arose from a different set of problems that the crisis exposed.

The commentary in this chapter begins in the leadup to the 2020 Presidential election in the United States, and takes in the various episodes through which the condition of democracy progressed from a runny nose to a raging, life-threatening fever.

5.1 Is freedom of speech a right to tell lies?

13 June 2020

We have become very tolerant of lying in the public conversation, and this has not served us well. Imagining ourselves able to detect the truth at the pub, we are led astray by demagogues. Is it time to regulate truth-telling? If so, when and how?

Certain facts make the (former) President of the United States uncomfortable.[4] He prefers "alternative facts." Ordinary folk, who lack the particular skills needed to rule an empire, would call them "lies."

In late May 2020, POTUS was expounding some alternative facts about the perils of voting by mail when his favourite platform had the temerity to put a warning notice on his tweet and direct readers to a fact-checking site. He denounced that action, saying that Twitter was "completely stifling free speech".

It would be a strange world indeed if promoters of the truth were the enemies of the United States Constitution. Does the Bill of Rights contain a right to tell lies? There is a legal answer to that question, no doubt, but I'd like to focus on the economics of lying. When do the costs of letting people say anything they like outweigh the benefits?

The right to lie, if it exists, is certainly not universal or unfettered. Judges can and do impose harsh penalties on witnesses who fail to tell the whole truth and nothing but the truth. Michael Flynn, a former advisor to POTUS, was up on perjury charges for (apparently) lying to a court when he plead guilty to having lied to the FBI. While he now asserts he did not lie to the FBI, his false confession has gotten him into a whole lot of bother that he could have avoided if he had stuck to the truth all along.

The scientific and medical professions are also unforgiving of deliberate falsehood. Sydney doctor William McBride achieved fame in the 1960s for alerting the world to the fact that morning sickness drug Thalidomide caused birth defects. However, several decades later, his work on Debendox resulted in his being struck off the medical register for deliberately falsifying data.[5] In science, as in court, there is an independent arbiter of truth and falsehood. There needs to be, because falsehood can do a lot of damage in those arenas.

In a less forensic setting like everyday life, things are a bit more relaxed. The law gives advertisers some leeway to make exaggerated claims or "puffery" to sell their products. The Federal Trade Commission of the United States usually does not prosecute puffery: *"The Commission generally will not pursue cases involving obviously exaggerated or puffing representations, i.e., those that the ordinary consumers do not take seriously."* [6] Here the defence is that any such lies are so obvious that no one would be deceived by them.

Finally we turn to the main game: political speech. As in the puffery case, bald-faced lies by politicians go unpunished. However, they do not always meet the FTC's criterion for exemption. These lies are not so obviously wrong that ordinary voters would see through them. In fact, there is a mountain of evidence that political lies can be highly persuasive.[7]

Also unlike puffery, it matters very much what voters think will be the consequence of voting this way or that. It is one thing to pick a chocolate chip cookie that turns out not to be the world's best. It is an entirely different thing to pick the wrong President. The disappointment lasts far longer and potentially reaches every part of your life.

The political arena has more in common with the courtroom, scientific and medical establishments as far as consequences of lying go. However, there is one crucial difference. In political speech, the regulatory authority has a conflict of interest. Political speech is unavoidably about the Government, so it is not practical to assign the job of policing truthfulness to that same Government.

You don't have to travel far to find examples of governments in the present day and age who use their power to suppress the public expression of sentiments that they find offensive. In 2015 two journalists were tried for a crime carrying a 7 year jail term: defaming the Thai navy by publishing a story about the alleged involvement of navy officers in human trafficking.[8] Encouragingly, they got off. However, the President of Egypt said in March 2018 that any media insult to the army or police is treason.[9] If you think he's kidding, take a closer look at the Peter Greste case.

Given the massive power imbalance, it seems more democratic to let the public, and journalists, say what they will and be prepared to put up with some occasional statements that might fail a polygraph test.

But what about the case of a government, especially a President, telling lies? Is that protected speech under the Constitution of anywhere? Should it be? Let's do a quick cost-benefit analysis of a proposal for independent oversight of the Government's truthfulness. We need to examine five possibilities:

1   No regulation of Government truthfulness
2   Government tells the truth and regulator approves of it
3   Government lies and regulator calls it out
4   Government tells the truth, but regulator cries wolf
5   Government lies and regulator approves of it.

Relative to possibility 1, the other four would involve the cost of the regulatory activity. This may not be small if a Government is frequently making public statements. However, the press seems to manage it on a shoestring, so the cost should not be exaggerated.

An unfettered and unaccountable Government could get up to a great deal of mischief, so the net disbenefit for possibility 1 could be large. To gauge how large that could be, one could look at the correlation between high per-capita GDP and the prevalence of democratic, as opposed to autocratic governments.[10] I note that correlation does not necessarily indicate causation. However in the cited article, I performed statistical analysis that suggests causation flows from democratisation to higher per capita GDP with a lag of perhaps a decade.

Possibilities 2 and 3 represent correct regulatory choices. Possibilities 4 and 5 represent the two types of regulatory error. While these erroneous possibilities could involve some large costs, they should arise infrequently if the regulator is competent and independent. As long as the error probability is low, the net benefit of regulating Government truthfulness should be strongly positive.

So, does the most powerful man in the world have a right to tell lies? Constitutional experts may think so, but this proposition fails a social cost-benefit test. An economist would say, tell the truth Mr President, and stop complaining about the accountability mechanism.

What happened since then

For the time being, Presidential lying is not the everyday occurrence that it was over the past four years. The current President is choosing not to exercise any constitutional right he might be thought to have to mislead or obfuscate.

That is certainly admirable, but it would be better to put the matter beyond doubt—to establish positively that powerful democratic rulers have a higher moral duty to be truthful. It should not depend on one individual's personal preferences. It means too much to all of us.

5.2 Prospects for a lie-detecting algorithm to apply to online news

31 Jan 2021

In the world of mathematical propositions, some are provable (true) and some are disprovable (false). But, troublingly, a vast number are neither provable nor disprovable. It isn't just that no one has yet had the patience or wisdom to resolve these limbo-land propositions. It is **impossible** to prove or disprove them. That is a proposition that has been proven. It is Godel's incompleteness theorem.[11]

The incompleteness of demonstrable truth and falsehood is an inauspicious start to the task of devising a way to find and destroy fake news. I mean news that really is fake and not just inconvenient to someone with a bullhorn. Nevertheless, we proceed because we must. We may not be able to get to the bottom of everything, but we may still be able to call out some howlers and reaffirm some useful, valid messages.

Where do you turn when humans can't be trusted?

To focus our efforts, let's look at the type of news that is most contentious: news about politics. This is one area where government regulation doesn't sit well. We're happy to have the government regulate product safety or pollution guidelines, but we are alarmed by the idea that the government would decide what people can say about the government itself. We can all see the regulator has a conflict of interest.

When you get right down to it, no one is really neutral when expressing an opinion about the government of the day. This is part of the attraction of getting a computer algorithm to help, if it can be done. There is some reason for hope.

Why I think that computers could do this

One example is the problem of redistricting—drawing the boundaries of electorates. The history of redistricting skulduggery is long and rich. From rotten boroughs in England to Gerrymandering in Massachusetts, many clever ruses have been concocted to allow minorities to achieve Parliamentary and Congressional majorities. In those cases, the problem was that the strategic decisions about boundary design were made by the same politicians who stood to gain by them. Fortunately, a mathematical solution to this conflict of interest problem is already available, if there is a will to use it. Scientifically-minded people have recognised for some time that fair redistricting could be done by a computer program. It turns out that there is a unique way of drawing electoral boundaries in any geographic area with an equal number of voters in each district, as long as the shapes of these districts are as convex as possible—ie, more like balloons or polygons and less like salamanders or writhing snakes. That's a math problem that can be solved without even asking which party the people in each district are likely to support. It is objective. The human element and conflict of interest can be removed by computer.

Another example is the method used by Google to find internet sites that provide objective, high quality information about any topic of interest. The Page-rank algorithm finds a way to cut through all the noise, chatter and misdirection to find authoritative sources—an impressive achievement in the present disinformation age. A key point here is that Google relies on the topology of the web to determine the reliability of information, not subjective judgements (or paid advertising). It is objective because Google doesn't even look at the information itself.

It's a bit like the military concept of signal intelligence—understanding an enemy's command and control structure simply by tracing the way signals propagate within their network in response to a spy-plane incursion. You don't know what they're saying, but you do know who they're saying it to. The chain of messages reveals the chain of command.

Analogously the Page-rank algorithm looks for and evaluates authorities (mavens) and hubs (connectors or referrers) on a topic. It does this purely by mapping the hyperlinks from one site to another. Authorities are sites that have lots of inbound links. Hubs are sites that have lots of outbound links.

But what's a good hub or authority? A good authority is one that is pointed to by good hubs, and a good hub is one that points to good authorities. Scientific citation indexes rely on the same concept.[12] If this chicken and egg problem sounds too hard to crack, mathematics has the answer, or rather two answers. This problem is really no harder than the problem of solving a system of n equations in n variables. In linear algebra, one way of solving this is to invert an n x n matrix. Of course, when n is more than 100 billion pages that type of computation is out of the question.

However, the other answer from mathematics is recursion: start with an approximation, calculate all the page ranks, then update the approximation and re-calculate all the page ranks. Iterate until the page ranks converge to stable values. Part of Page and Brin's genius was that they found a way to solve this complex system of simultaneous equations using a fairly simple recursive technique that is well within a modern computer's capability and converged quickly.

Given that success, it does not seem too much of a stretch to think that a similar type of algorithm can help us to find truthful news, or at least to evaluate the reliability of information from any particular source. A reliable news outlet is really little different from a good authority on the web. A reliable media guide is really little different from a good hub.

For a third example that looks further into the deep space of tech possibility, there may be a variant of blockchain techniques that could help to verify the chain of custody of certain high-value news. This technology is already being used to validate a host of official records, including but not limited to bank transactions. As the unit costs fall, the scope of possible application of the method increases. Maybe real news will be blockchain-validated back to original sources in future? Fake news could be red-flagged automatically because the certificates would be invalid. In an era where deepfake videos are becoming a problem, this type of solution could come into its own.

Clearly, there's a long way to go and much to debate concerning the limits of free speech. I've hoped to show you in this brief note that the many conflicts of interest could plausibly be addressed through intelligent use of computer technology and mathematics. Many of the ideas that would be needed exist now and have been implemented in relevant settings.

As to the objectivity of computers, I don't pretend that algorithms are value-neutral. It's just that you can usually see what the assumptions are and what values are embedded in them. You can then make your own choices about whether to accept the advice and how to correct for any inherent biases.

The examples in this article are explained in more detail in the last two chapters.

5.3 Should we trust capitalists to keep democracy strong?

26 Jan 2021

Milton Friedman directly linked capitalism to political freedom in his 1962 book. The idea was that economic freedom (delivered by capitalism) was necessary but not sufficient for political freedom. Friedman met with Chilean President Pinochet two years after the military junta came to power and it was reported in 1975 that the Pinochet government was acting on Friedman's economic policy advice. The interpretation of those facts, ie whether Friedman's intervention had pro- or anti-democratic effects, has been much disputed since then.

Much more recently, a host of major US corporations have

announced the suspension of political donations to congressmen who voted to oppose certification of the Electoral College's votes for President Biden. Similar boycotts have been proposed for some blatantly untruthful news outlets. Will that work? Most likely, if the corporations hold their line. After all, money talking is the new freedom of speech.

Dominion Voting Systems has succeeded in doing something that no amount of reasoned debate ever could have—silenced Rudy Giuliani and Sidney Powell, and elicited humiliating retractions from Fox News hosts and others. They did this with standard corporate tools— defamation suits and the threat of enormous financial consequences.

Recent experience suggests that capitalism may have an effective role to play in keeping democracy on the rails. For me, I must say it is a surprising turn of events. When I read Orwell's 1984, I was in no doubt that Big Brother represented a monopolistic corporation and I was left with no hope that free markets would free the people.

Then when the year 1984 actually arrived, I found myself in an auditorium in Cupertino California where Apple unveiled its Macintosh computer. To get the crowd of shareholders in the mood, the organisers played a film clip that alluded to Orwell's novel. Apple's chief rival, IBM, was painted as Big Brother, the bringer of blue mass conformity. The Mac provided the spark for an individualistic uprising.

Casting these themes into the dying days of the Trump experiment, the role reversals are happening so quickly it is hard to keep track. The rugged individual patriots, not content with destroying IBM made their move on the Capitol. The conspiracy they fought was so vast, so comprehensive that it had erased every shred of evidence of wrongdoing. The conspirators were so adept at reasoning and deploying facts that it was dangerous to listen to them. The latter-day Minutemen appeared confident they would get pardons, so they threw caution to the wind.

All of a sudden, Apple and IBM found something they could agree on: anarchy was bad for business. If it was possible to overthrow a 200 year old elected government by force, then the rule of law would no longer prevail. To a corporation, one of the most important aspects of the rule of law is the protection of property rights. Milton Friedman put it like this:

> *I think that nothing is so important for freedom as recognizing in the law each individual's natural right to property ...*[13]

As the dust settles on the January 6th storming of Congress, the 'patriots' wake up to discover their pardons aren't coming. The hard core activists retreat into the darkest most encrypted corners of the web to lick their wounds and attempt reorganisation. Many followers will find a different, hopefully more constructive activity to focus their time and energies upon. With a bit of luck, the mania will fade away.

We can take some comfort that business is capable of acting decisively in a moment of crisis, even if the political class is not. But let's not kid ourselves. Property rights motivate them, not your right to free expression or political freedom.

What happened since then

Too early to say.

5.4 Why it might be rational for Republicans to shoot themselves in the foot

9 Feb 2021

Pre-trial punditry about how Republican senators may vote in the second impeachment trial got me wondering whether game theory could help to understand the puzzling situation these senators find themselves in.

On one hand, many have more or less admitted the obvious: that Trump intentionally caused the January 6 insurrection. Many recognise that their own presidential aspirations would be more likely to succeed if Trump was convicted and banned from holding public office. Also, they probably understand that the party may be more viable in future if it rejects the anti-logic minoritarian agenda promoted by the former president.

However, all seem to recognise that going against that agenda in a public way risks alienating the party's most ardent supporters. Their own immediate re-electoral prospects may be snuffed out if they antagonise the base. A likely outcome is that all or most choose the least desirable option, despite the availability of a win-win alternative.

This type of situation is not unheard of in politics or human affairs more broadly. It sounds a lot like the classic Prisoners Dilemma problem from game theory, which is also ubiquitous in economics. Let's probe whether that story fits the facts.

Imagine for the moment that you are a Republican senator. You have two strategy options, which we'll call "stop the steal!" and "accept the result." The other player in this game is the rest of the Grand Old Party, and the Rest of Party (ROP) has the same two strategy options.

Constructing a payoff matrix involves a bit of speculation and subjective judgement, but if we accept the ranking of outcomes mentioned above, we can take a stab at it.

Payoff matrix

		You	
		Stop the steal!	**Accept the result**
ROP	**Stop the steal!**	**You:** Small loss	**You:** Large loss
		ROP: Small loss	**ROP:** Large gain
	Accept the result	**You:** Large gain	**You:** Medium gain
		ROP: Large loss	**ROP:** Medium gain

Clearly, everyone would be better off if both players chose to accept the result, compared to the outcome if both players chose to stop the steal.

However, it would not be rational for you to choose to accept the result given the payoff rankings in the matrix.

There are two things that player ROP could do. If ROP chooses stop the steal, then your payoff would be better by choosing to also stop the steal (you'd get a small loss instead of a large loss).

If ROP chooses to accept the result, then your payoff would still be better by choosing to stop the steal (you'd get a large gain instead of a medium gain).

In game theory parlance, we'd say that 'stop the steal' is a dominant strategy for you. The payoffs are symmetric, so it is a dominant strategy for ROP also. That means rational players would make the choice that leaves everyone worse off.

Does game theory tell us how to get a better outcome? Yes. It can be done if the rules of the game are tweaked. One solution might be to convert this one-shot game into a repeated game. While an impeachment trial is unlikely to recur frequently, it is part of a long-running series of tests for a political party being pulled in two different directions. The choice of whether to give in to populism or to adhere to longstanding Republican party values will present itself many times and in many different guises.

A player who knows that the game will be repeated may choose differently this time. Simulations and contests with real people have shown that a strategy called "tit-for-tat" can be highly successful in moving players towards the superior cooperative outcome. In tit-for-tat, you cooperate (accept the result) until the other player defects (stop the steal). If and when that happens, you defect to punish the other player until she returns to cooperation, at which point you do, too.

Another solution is to breach one of the key rules of the game by discussing your likely choices with the other player. In the classic Prisoners Dilemma, two suspects in a crime are interrogated separately by the police and offered inducements to confess. If the suspects were allowed to confer before responding to those inducements, they would realise that the police case is weak and they can both do better by refusing to confess.

Something similar is possible in the Republican dilemma. These senators could agree to accept the result / convict / disown Qanon / embrace science / take climate change seriously and thereby set their party on a more sustainable course for the future. To solve a collective action problem like that, some catalysing leadership would be required.

What happened since then

As everyone now knows, on February 13, 2021, the Republican senators largely voted to acquit Donald Trump, private citizen, in his second impeachment trial. Two things about that result were interesting. First, the Republican bloc was not completely unified. Seven Republicans voted to convict, meaning that a majority of votes were against Trump, but it was insufficient for the required supermajority.

Second, many of those Republican senators voting to acquit did not assert that he was innocent of the charges. Instead, they relied on the technical argument that as he was no longer President the conviction would have no practical effect. The former Senate majority leader more or less admitted that Trump had done what he was accused of doing.

5.5 Is the sensible centre empty?

5 March 2020

One hears that the lefties have taken over the public broadcaster. To provide a fair balance, the fear-mongerers advocate loudly for a world where Plutocrats tell everyone what to do. The reasonable person on the Clapham Omnibus has nowhere left to stand. Surely this is not how it was meant to be?

If you can imagine a curve in the shape of a bell—like the Liberty Bell but without the crack—you will see how peoples' preferences are usually arranged. Most people are in the middle, where the curve is high. There are a lot fewer people at the extreme left and right edges. This curve illustrates how democracy was meant to work. Everybody votes according to their preferences and we wind up with something that a lot of people want and that very few people are desperately unhappy with.

Unfortunately, it seems that peoples' preferences have changed now. The curve now looks like two bells set so far apart from each other that they don't overlap at all. Now, voting produces an outcome that half the people will always be desperately unhappy with. It is also an unstable outcome because if the unhappy people get the upper hand next time, the people in charge and the rules they make will change to something very very different from now.

You may well ask whether this is a problem? After all, we don't all want the same beverages, clothing styles or haircuts. Different tastes make the world an interesting place. By diversifying, we strengthen society. Why not here?

Well, it is a problem because in politics, everyone has to have the same thing. I can't have a conservative national leader while you have a progressive one. We all have to have the same leader, and we all have to follow the same laws, administered by the same bureaucrats.

One solution would be to split into two separate nations. Lefties to the West and conservatives to the East. Alternatively, Lefties in the coastal megacities and Righties in the agricultural heartland. Lefties and Righties might not agree on the laws that govern their local behaviour, but they might not need to do that. Different cultures still seem to be able to trade with each other.

I have to say that the history of partitions like this is not a source of encouragement,[14] but let's not rule it out entirely. If there is a geographic dimension to the split, then partition may be easier to bring about without massive property disputes. Of course, it all gets harder if one group occupies resource-rich territory and the other group doesn't.

Another solution is available, although I hesitate to mention it because it is so revolutionary. Perhaps people on opposite sides of the preference curve could speak and listen to each other about their concerns and values. The challenges of living together as a single society could be treated as a problem that everyone needs to solve. We could take the view that the problem is not solved until everyone believes the solution is acceptable, if not ideal. Finally, and most radically, we could listen to what facts and logic suggest we should do. Rather than shut out inconvenient messages that pass a basic truth test, perhaps we should take the view that the problem is not solved until these messages have been incorporated in the answer.

The sensible centre is looking pretty vacant right now, but when the stakes are high and we all have to do the same thing, it is in everyone's interest to move into that space.

What happened since then

The new POTUS differs from the old one in several important respects. Among those, President Biden has made a serious effort to occupy the sensible centre. Arguably, his electoral success in November 2020 owes much to this centrist strategy.

The increasingly desperate tactics that ex-President Trump employed to remain in power despite electoral defeat suggest that his alternative strategy of pandering to extreme anti-establishmentarians planted the seeds of its own destruction. It is worth taking a moment to outline those tactics.

Pre-election, he made a concerted, but clumsy effort to conflate candidate Biden with a Ukrainian corruption scandal, leading to his own first impeachment. He resisted the expansion of absentee and pre-poll voting that the pandemic had made necessary. He did that because he correctly intuited that those votes were far more likely to be against him.

While votes were being counted, he claimed victory and asserted that illegal voting and election tampering was reducing his margin. These claims were strenuously denied and debunked by a raft of public officials from his own party at Federal and State levels.

Once the writing was on the wall and it was plain to all that he had lost, he launched a large number of court actions at State and Federal level, even reaching to the Supreme Court trying to invalidate the votes that went against him. None of these helped his cause.

In a scandalous telephone call with the Georgia Secretary of State, he asked that official to overturn the results of the election in that state. The call was released publicly.

He publicly called for the Vice President, Republican senators and congressmen to object to the electoral college votes that went against him, setting the stage, he hoped, for a one state one vote determination of the outcome.

Most outrageous of all, when all of those avenues were closed to him, he incited a large mob to take over the Capitol building by force and thereby halt the count that he would lose. The immediate threat of bodily harm that entailed was too much even for his most ardent party members.

All of these considerations imply that the sensible centre is not empty. It was just temporarily vacant while we all waited for people to calm down. Eventually, we hope, the central tendency will be re-established.

PART 3

MISUNDERSTANDING THE FUTURE

New Zealand is the home of hokey-pokey ice cream. A majority of New Zealanders think it's great, but the people who like it best are mostly in the South Island. The people in the North Island can take it or leave it. Let's say there are 3 million people in the North Island and only 49% of them like hokey-pokey. In contrast, there are 1 million people in the South Island and 70% of them like it. On a whole country vote, the pro-hokey-pokey party would win government with 2.17 million votes out of 4 million.

If the pro-pistachio ice cream faction took control of the redistricting process, then things could turn out quite differently. The country might be split into two electoral districts: North and South Islands. Being more populous, the North Island would get three members of parliament and the South Island only one. The South Island seat would be filled with a hokey-pokey party person, but all three North Island seats would be narrowly won by the pistachio party. When it came to a vote in parliament, hokey-pokey would lose 3–1.

There is a long history of electoral shenanigans, which is pretty funny when it doesn't affect you. There were the rotten boroughs in England which allowed a small number of people to obtain a puppet in parliament. That is called malapportionment. However, even when the number of voters in each district is equal, there is still plenty that can go wrong.

Governor Elbridge Gerry of Massachusetts made a name for himself and his methods by designing district boundaries in such a way that his detractors were concentrated in a small number of electorates, while his supporters were scattered across the remaining electorates to achieve a small majority in each one. The result of his handiwork was that a district in Essex County was so contorted that it resembled a salamander.

Clearly, this isn't cricket, but what can you do? How does direct democracy solve this problem? It may not. When voting is by district, you have to solve this problem before you can even start to have direct democracy.

Luckily, this is something that can be done quite easily with geometry and a computer program. You start by deciding how many districts there will be. Then you divide the voting population by the number of districts to determine how many voters there must be in each one. Finally, you use a computer program to divide up the territory into the right number of districts so that each one has about the right number of voters, subject to one further rule. All of the districts must be convex polygons, allowing for natural boundaries like coastlines, mountain ranges and rivers.

The key insight is that a unique electoral map emerges from these rules. There is no possibility of fiddling it. Like some, but not all other decisions, this one is best kept out of the hands of politicians and voters. A computer will be fairer and more consistent.

The idea is simple, but the details are a bit mathematical. Rather than go further into it here, I will just point you to a newspaper article where the idea of compact electorates is explained and shown in map form:

https://www.washingtonpost.com/news/wonk/
wp/2016/01/13/this-is-actually-what-america-would-look-
like-without-gerrymandering/?utm_term=.ed9e47c13a02

The redistricting function of politicians is clearly one that should be taken out of their hands. A computer would do a better job and democracy would better reflect the will of voters if it did. We may still need politicians to make some decisions, but this is not one of them.

Lobbying as an investment

So far we've talked about how electronic voting could make direct democracy workable and about redistricting by computer, but we haven't really explained why we want direct democracy in the first place. We'll do that here.

The biggest argument for direct democracy is that politicians are very vulnerable to lobbying. Lobbying, you will recall, is a form of propaganda intended to make politicians act against the public interest. Lobbyists have various methods, which I won't go into here. Most of these are within the law, but morally questionable. Rather than focus on the moral issues, I'd like to look at the economics of lobbying.

Lobbyists must spend money to achieve their purposes. They must compete with other lobbyists who may want the politicians to do something different or to do a favour for a different group of cashed-up meddlers. Lobbying is an investment made by competing firms.

It is a high risk, high reward investment. We hear all the time about a campaign donation of as little as $10,000 by a firm that later gets a concession from government worth millions. But we also hear about political donors who don't get what they want even when their candidate gets elected. We sometimes hear about lobbyists or politicians who wind up in jail. Usually, nothing can be proven, but we remain suspicious.

If we had direct democracy, this is one thing we wouldn't have to worry about as much. It would just be too expensive to bribe a majority of all the voters. Here is perhaps the strongest reason for direct democracy. Could it work?

Will voters connect the dots?

Let us imagine that we have a completely direct democracy. People use some form of fingerprint/retinal scan protected Facebook account to vote on every single question of government. We might need to vote every day, but we could do it in the evening after dinner.

We might need to make sure we don't vote while we're watching the news or current affairs on TV because we might do something impulsive that has lasting consequences.

There would be heightened stress around budget time. People are quite likely to vote for lower taxes and better government services, but that would eventually drive the government broke if the budget never gets balanced. We might vote to default on our nation's debts, because that would solve a few problems for now.

We might be tempted to vote to pick on some minority group that we don't like. We might respond to news about terrorism by voting to take rights away from Muslims. We might change our minds frequently.

In short, there is a real danger we would run the country the way a child would. Our allies might wonder how reliable we are, and our enemies might see an opportunity to exploit a lack of leadership. Where would that steadying parental influence come from? In most governments, that would be the public service. They are the people who are supposed to know what they're doing.

Politicians have many shortcomings, but one thing you can say for them is that they know how to work with the public service. How would a large group of electronic voters do that? Sadly for the idea of direct democracy, I think it wouldn't work. It is hard enough to supervise a public service department with a conventional congressional committee. The idea of a "committee" of millions of voters doing anything effective is beyond far-fetched.

One final problem with direct democracy: who decides what questions are voted on, when they are put to a vote, and how exactly the questions are asked? A single person or a small committee must do that important work. One might as well call that person and those committee members politicians, because that is what they would be. There is no getting around it.

More modest ideas for reform

Let's not despair. Perhaps we can set our sights a bit lower and aim for a more modest improvement. Leaving aside the redistricting function, which should certainly be automated, if it's true that the problems of running the country like adults, managing the public service, and choosing the questions we vote on are beyond direct democracy, can we improve on the way representative democracy works?

Here we confront the challenge of political parties, because most decisions of government are actually made by them. In fact, these decisions are made by the political party that holds the majority of seats in parliament. In the case of America, it is the White House, where one seat is enough for a majority. Most of the time, the votes in parliaments and congresses are foregone conclusions that simply formalise the decisions prepared earlier in the party room.

This probably wasn't intended by the founding fathers of any country. Most constitutions fail to mention the existence of political parties. Nevertheless, that is where we are. We could try to ban political parties, but it might be more effective to regulate them instead.

Parties rely on donations from benefactors to conduct their business. This dependence is troubling, because these benefactors will obviously expect something in return. To the average voter, who may not have made any donations, favours to campaign donors look a lot like corruption.

We could ban party donations, but then the politicians would say that democracy can't function without them. We can and do regulate donations to some extent but really, who are we kidding? Money buys access to politicians. This just means that donors can have a private meeting with a politician and tell them how the donors would like them to vote on issues that affect them. This type of behaviour is protected under a misguided notion of free speech. Meanwhile the majority of voters, who can't afford to say anything, have to put up with bad policies and laws.

The obvious starting point is to ask how much money a political party needs and what it uses that money for. How do we know they couldn't do it for less money—meaning less exposure to corruption opportunities? Why is it acceptable for parties to refuse to disclose their finances? What rate of return do their donors earn on their donations? If political parties are the price of a working democracy, what is an efficient price for that service? Could some other group of people provide it for a lower cost?

We could do worse than to apply some market discipline to this shady area where inefficiency and ignorance invite impropriety.

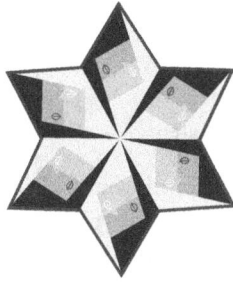

7

WHAT WE CAN DO FOR OURSELVES

Whether we are able to dispense with politicians or not, we will need to get more involved in the important decisions of government. Outsourcing these tasks has been like taking bickering children out of the back seat of the car and letting them fight for control of the steering wheel. In this chapter I'd like to talk about a few things we can do that would help us with our situation. There are three parts to this viewpoint.

First, we have a preoccupation with threats to our security that is enabled by our passive response to political messages and driven to prominence by leaders who have put their own interests ahead of ours. We can make more use of science to understand threats better and determine effective responses. We can build coalitions with other people to reduce the cost of eliminating threats.

Second, we have a tendency to see conspiracies everywhere we look, and that shapes our attitudes to our fellow citizens in a counterproductive way. Most conspiracy theories are a mis-diagnosis. Actually, true conspiracies are rare and, as any antitrust economist will tell you, holding a secret cartel together is much more difficult than you might think. What if the world we see is actually the result of uncoordinated choices by hapless individuals responding to a perverse incentive scheme? In that case, the point of leverage is to change the incentive scheme.

Third, we long for a trusted adviser that knows what's really going on and is honest (and caring) enough to tell us. There is no shortage of advice givers, but how do we find one we can trust—especially now in the age of information overload, where malicious agents run riot? Google doesn't have the answer, but we may be able to find it if we study their methods.

7.1 Threats and security

When your safety is threatened, you don't sit down and read a good book. Not even one that might help you to solve your problems. There is a sense of urgency that tends to rule out a thoughtful response. If you are reading this book now, then hopefully you have some breathing space before the next attack. Let's use it to examine threats in a theoretical way while we have the chance to ponder our alternatives.

Broadly speaking, there are two possible responses to a threat: defence and attack. You can shield yourself and your loved ones behind strong defences, or you can take on the enemy and try to eliminate the threat once and for all. Let's call these responses 'taking shelter' and 'threat elimination.' These names are a bit narrow for describing the full range of possible defensive and offensive situations, but we need a handle and these are short, sweet and mainly to the point.

Whether taking shelter or threat elimination is the best strategy for you depends on the situation. For example, in a tornado you'd be better off taking shelter than trying to fight the wind, but to protect yourself from malaria you'd be better off eliminating the mosquitoes than hiding under nets and drinking quinine.

Your choice of strategy should rationally depend on which one costs you the least. Here, cost is meant to be taken in a broad sense. It's not just money, but also the discomfort, inconvenience, foregone alternatives, risk of sickness and death of yourself and your loved ones that also come into the calculation.

The cost of a taking shelter strategy depends on the number of people who are under the shadow of a particular threat. The more people that need shelter, the more it costs. The costs of a threat elimination strategy have a somewhat different profile. For any particular type of threat, these costs tend to be fixed. The cost of running a rogue elephant out of the village doesn't depend on the number of people living there.

By looking only at costs, we can deduce that threat elimination becomes more attractive and taking shelter less attractive as the number of affected people is increased, provided of course that the people can act in a coordinated way. The more people that join in the plan to repel the rogue elephant, the smaller the cost (the risk of getting trampled or gored with a tusk) that each one faces.

The costs of both a taking shelter and threat elimination strategy increase with the number of different types of threats. However, it is often true that many different types of threats have a common weakness, and we can exploit it to make security less costly. For example, there are a great many food and water-borne germs that can make you sick or kill you, but almost all of them can be eliminated by cooking your food, boiling your water and washing your hands before you eat. Many threats, and one simple method of eliminating them. This efficiency is brought to us by science and understanding the things that threaten us.

Why your leaders might prefer to defend

Terrorism is in the news a lot lately. The motivations of terrorists are puzzling to most of us. It is hard to conceive of a rational purpose behind these attacks. The fact that terror attacks in the first world are mostly launched by autonomous 'lone wolf' perpetrators is highly significant. There is no centralised enemy that we can go and bomb. Even if we had the stomach for a fight, we wouldn't know where to send the troops.

We know next to nothing about our enemies, and for all these reasons we are virtually forced to defend. So we put bollards around our government buildings and concrete barriers across public promenades. We force technology companies to design back-entrances to encrypted communication channels so the government can eavesdrop on all our conversations and financial transactions. We suspend ancient civil rights like habeas corpus, a speedy trial, and the right to face your accuser. We make our world more Orwellian in the aftermath of every terror attack.

I am not the first person to notice that these changes can be quite convenient for a nation's political leaders. Not just for fighting terror, but also for fighting legitimate political rivals. Even if one were inclined not to be so cynical, this defensive posture towards terrorism has the advantage for a government that it gives them something important and urgent to do and a reason to demand extra tax revenue. That is probably something that both sides of politics can agree on.

Have we been too quick to settle on a taking shelter strategy for terrorism? Could we do more to eliminate the threat? I don't know the answer to these questions, but I think it is important that we keep asking them.

One thing occurs to me, though. Let us say that there was a viable threat elimination strategy available. Would our political leaders vigorously pursue it? The answer to that question depends on a cost and benefit calculation that these leaders most likely do on a frequent basis. This calculation is a little more complex than the one that society as a whole would do. Society will just compare the costs of taking shelter with those of eliminating the threat, and go for the least cost option.

The political calculus is not a cost minimisation exercise. Rather, their question will be whether the regime is made more durable and profitable (for them) by directing resources towards coexistence with threats or towards eliminating them? On one hand, a problem solver with no more problems to solve becomes obsolete. On the other hand, a leader with too many problems to solve will get replaced by someone more proactive.

As with most problems in economics, there is likely to be a point of equilibrium—a sweet spot where some threats get eliminated and others are allowed to fester away in the background. A benign social planner might have chosen a different balancing point and, for the reasons just mentioned, that point is likely to be one where more threats are eliminated, fewer resources are required to maintain the peace, and fewer intrusions on individual liberties seem necessary.

What you can do

We don't need to be passive victims in this coliseum. After all, we choose our political leadership. We can try to improve our understanding of the threats we face by studying them. Rather than getting distracted by the emotive images of scattered corpses and smashed buildings, we can try to understand the motivations, methods and vulnerabilities of perpetrators who, at the end of the day, are pursuing political strategies.

We can take the trouble to learn about scientific disciplines that are relevant to the threats we face, whether that is climatology, psychology, molecular biology, astronomy or economics. We can interrogate the experts the government puts forward to convince us of their point of view, and put some discipline on these experts to be diligent and frank.

Where some form of collective action is needed to eliminate a threat, work on building coalitions yourself. These could be coalitions of friends and neighbours to reinforce the importance of vaccination, or coalitions of professionals to reinforce the importance of scientific results for particular problems.

7.2 A vast conspiracy?

The conservatives in most first world countries are convinced that there is a vast conspiracy among progressives and leftists—particularly in the media—to deceive the public and thereby achieve a tyranny of moral choices that most right-thinking God-fearing people would oppose. This conspiracy might take the form of a cadre of lefty journalists inhabiting a loosely policed state-funded public broadcasting organisation. It might take the form of a "deep state" lurking within the public service that remains loyal to some long-deposed national leader.

The progressives in most first world countries are convinced that there is a vast conspiracy among monied interests—particularly among those who have inherited their vast fortunes—to deceive the public and thereby achieve a tyranny of business monopolies that keeps the oligarchs powerful and the average person dependent and compliant. This conspiracy might take the form of the corruption of politicians needing campaign funding to remain in office. It might take the form of insidious infiltration of reputable educational institutions who reluctantly flirt with disreputable ideas and their advocates in order to fund their operations.

I am not here to say which of these theories is right. Probably they are both wrong. I'd like to explore what it takes to make a conspiracy successful and whether these conditions are likely to be sustainable.

This matters because if there is a conspiracy, then the solution is to attack it, expose the conspirators and thereby undo the damage that they've caused. However, if there is actually no conspiracy then the solution is something quite different. Instead of attacking people who may not actually have any idea of the consequences of their decisions, a more effective intervention would be to change their incentives.

OPEC

Not all commodities are equally important. One among them, oil, has a particular strategic importance since virtually all mechanised transport, from airplanes to tuk-tuks needs it. Natural gas, which is a byproduct of oil extraction, is also a strategic commodity since most of Europe needs it to keep warm in the winter and a large part of industry uses it, or oil, as fuel. Stop the flow of oil, and the economy stops.

Many countries have oil deposits, but most industrialised countries need to import it because they don't produce enough. There is a handful of countries that are net exporters of oil. What would happen if these countries formed a conspiracy to control the flow of export oil? We found out in 1973. The conspiracy, called the Organisation of the Petroleum Exporting Countries, or OPEC, restricted the supply of oil to the USA in that year (for political rather than economic reasons at that time). It was a tectonic shift in the global balance of political power. The West's dependence on imported oil was shown to be a strategic vulnerability. The favourable endowments of oil in the Middle East and other OPEC member countries gave them strategic leverage.

In economic terms, OPEC is a cartel. Most cartels operate under the radar because they are prohibited by the laws of most developed countries. This makes it difficult to observe what they do. OPEC is able to operate openly because it is an international agreement among sovereign states, and there are no international equivalents to antitrust or anti-cartel laws. We can learn something about how cartels operate by observing OPEC's behaviour, but we must turn to economic theory to understand secret, illicit cartels.

The goal of a business cartel is to extract monopoly profits. This is easier for an actual monopoly to do, because the owner can command the employees to reduce output in a very specific way so that prices rise to the exact level that maximises profits. For a cartel this is harder because there is a club of owners, and they may not all agree to the individual output reductions that would be needed to maximise the profits of the group.

If we look at the membership of OPEC in the 1980s, it is understandable why some of these countries may have had trouble agreeing on business rules. Two of the members, Iran and Iraq, were at war with each other for most of that decade. More conventionally, but quite generally, cartels are intrinsically unstable because they are essentially agreements between competitors. Competitors have opposing interests. There is a constant tension between the collective benefit achieved by cooperating and the individual benefit that could be achieved by going rogue.

If a cartel member can secretly "cheat" on the cartel agreement, the potential payoffs can be large. Most cartel members agree to restrict their output in order to increase prices. If one member breaks that agreement and sells more than its quota, it can exploit the high prices to improve its financial position.

Over its history, several countries have left OPEC because they could not agree to the individual output restrictions that the group decided to impose. Nevertheless, OPEC has been durable as an institution, but its effectiveness in keeping oil prices high has waxed and waned. A recent problem for many members has been that as other national revenue sources falter and the cost of governing rises, they need to increase oil production just to balance the budget. For many of these countries, the profit-maximising oil price would involve an unacceptable budget deficit. For this reason we have seen a steep decline in crude oil prices since about 2014.

The 1919 World Series

The most infamous conspiracy in baseball was a shambolic affair. The White Sox players who were in on the scheme bumbled their way to a one game to four series deficit, according to plan. However, as the crucial fifth loss loomed, the conspirators seemed to have a change of heart. Suddenly they started playing better, and won the next two games. Reportedly they had become suspicious that their bookmaker friends would renege on the deal. It was only in the eighth game that the White Sox conspirators capitulated—and this may have been the result of threats of gangland violence.

What can we learn from this conspiracy? There are many tensions among the participants in a conspiracy. One conspirator can often do better for himself by surreptitiously cheating on the agreement. The need for secrecy makes it hard for cartel members to observe everything that is done by the others. The illegality of the enterprise makes it harder to punish cheaters, even when they are detected. There are certainly no legal avenues available for such punishment, and law enforcement mechanisms can't be used for this purpose.

Detection of cheating is a particular problem in a setting such as a sporting match. Did the batter strike out intentionally, or was it just good pitching? Did the fielder just trip accidentally or fall on purpose? Did the pitcher mean to walk the batter? It's very hard to tell.

Many other conspiracies suffer from similar enforcement problems, and this is one of the reasons that real conspiracies are so rare. Where they do exist, and some certainly do, they are often unstable and ineffective in the long run for the reasons we've just been talking about.

Another point about conspiracies worth emphasising is that they are never vast. In the Black Sox example, the whole team wasn't in on it, just a handful of players in key positions. OPEC currently has only 14 members. There is a very good reason for keeping conspiracies small. Apart from the obvious point that with more conspirators, the monopoly profit must be shared between more people, size increases risks. The bigger the group, the more likely someone will go rogue by cheating or by revealing the plot to the authorities. It's harder to monitor the behaviour of members of a larger group. A large cartel is more likely to have divergent interests and will be harder to discipline. Effective conspiracies are small.

Hapless individuals, not evil conspirators

The idea that our problems are caused by a conspiracy is superficially attractive. It suggests that a simple solution might be just around the corner. As a bonus, it creates opportunities to criticise other groups in society that we don't like.

By analysing OPEC, the Black Sox conspirators and the dynamics of cartels generally, I hope to have persuaded you of an important point. While conspiracies undoubtedly exist in various places around the world, it is exceedingly unlikely that they are pervasive, strategic, durable or even effective for any significant length of time.

If our problems are not caused by some vast conspiracy, then the countermeasure of exposing the conspiracy and busting the cartel will not be effective. Pursuing that course would delay meaningful action on solutions that would.

These alternative countermeasures are not so easy to implement. They involve altering the rules of society's main systems in ways that will alter the incentives faced by individuals who do the things we wish they wouldn't. There are no easy fixes here, so this is not such an attractive path. Still, it is better to persist at something difficult than to opt for something that is easy but pointless.

7.3 Where's Walter?

Who will tell us what's really going on? Between 1962 and 1981, the answer would have been Walter Cronkite. Walter was the anchor of CBS evening news on television for that whole time. Through the trauma of the Vietnam War, Kennedy's assassination, Watergate, the OPEC oil embargo, and the Iranian embassy hostages, as well as the excitement of the moon landing, Walter was there to answer our questions and keep us calm as the world trembled.

Since that time, we have not been so well served by television news anchors. In fact, the situation has gotten right out of hand. Believe it or not, some people make up stories that sound like news but are untrue. Well, actually, some people have always done that. The difference this time is that some of those people manage to broadcast their fabricated tales to a large audience on a daily basis. Sometimes they do this by tricking overworked editors into believing a bogus source. Other times they are acting on instructions from the head of the network.

We realise, belatedly, that the integrity of the news system is very dependent on the integrity of individual journalists and editors, and that integrity is under threat from the financial collapse of the existing business model for news. That model relied on advertising to pay for the news. Advertisers have found a more effective way to engage with the people who might buy their product. This engagement no longer relies on general-purpose broadcasts to everyone in a wide audience. It is much more individual, personalised and, in that sense, creepier.

Walter's passed on and, even if he were alive today, I'm not sure we would all listen to him in quite the same way. The times have changed. We must look somewhere else for a new authority on the questions that matter to us. We must look in a different way for these new authorities.

My purpose here is not to make you feel depressed. In fact, the internet which has enabled these creepy new advertisers to invade your privacy in unthinkable new ways has also enabled us to find authoritative advice on any topic we can name in an unexpected new way. That's what this section is about.

Signal intelligence

Let's begin to explore this unexpected new way by considering something that the military calls "signal intelligence." The basic idea is that you can tell quite a lot about what people are communicating without understanding any of the content of that communication. You walk through a forest and the birds around you start singing to each other suddenly. You don't know what they're saying, but you know they're talking about you.

You bump into a waiter in a crowded restaurant in Budapest and he spills his tray. Several goulash-spattered customers strike up an animated conversation with you in an unfamiliar tongue. You don't understand the words, but you have a pretty good idea what point they're trying to make.

A spy plane strays into Russian airspace and a nearby air force base sends a radio signal. The signal is encoded and perhaps the pilot doesn't speak Russian, but she knows the base commander is talking to his commander about her plane. If the intrusion seems threatening enough, her air force might be able to tell quite a lot about the whole Russian chain of command by following the pattern of radio signals. That is the intelligence that is gleaned from the signals alone.

Let's think about the internet. Perhaps you can tell something about how reliable the information on a web page is by looking at nothing other than the pattern of hyperlinks in and out of that web page and the link patterns of the pages that link to it? If you could do that, then a computer program could evaluate the reliability of web pages. Think how much time that would save and how objective the answers would be. Can it be done? Yes. It already has been.

Science citations

Long before the internet became a thing, scientists had developed a way to tell which journal articles they should read and which ones would be a waste of time. It is all about citations. If your article, published ten years ago, has 2,000 citations then it is probably a more important article than mine, also published ten years ago, which has none. There are 2,000 other published scientific articles that relied in some way on the work that you did in your article. None of these were written by yourself or any of your relatives who are not scientists. That gives your article quite a lot of credibility.

Now web pages are a bit like journal articles and hyperlinks are a bit like citations, but there is one important difference. Scientific journal articles are an example of a well controlled collection, meaning that before anyone can post an article, they must jump the hurdle of peer review. The majority of articles submitted, even by recognised academics, fail to clear this hurdle.

In contrast, the world wide web is uncontrolled. Computer scientists Sergey Brin and Larry Page[16] expressed the difference like so:

Another big difference between the web and traditional well controlled collections is that there is virtually no control over what people can put on the web. Couple this flexibility to publish anything with the enormous influence of search engines to route traffic and companies which deliberately manipulating search engines for profit become a serious problem. This problem that has not been addressed in traditional closed information retrieval systems.

These scientists could easily have been talking about the problem of extracting accurate, fact-checked news from the galaxy of echo chambers that we call the infotainment media. However, as you've probably guessed by now, they were talking about their ingenious solution to the internet search engine problem. Their solution was so ingenious that the company that brings it to your desktop is now one of the most profitable on Earth.

Maybe something similar to their solution can be used to find authoritative information in the vast, uncontrolled blogosphere?

Before the Page Rank algorithm

Page and Brin were not the first to think of studying the topology of the web to identify authorities. In trying to take this idea into the realm of news about politics and economics, it may be helpful to look at some of these earlier ideas which may translate more easily.

Let's start with the notion of hubs and authorities, which was explored in detail by Jon Kleinberg in 1998. Identify a particular subject area and by doing a text search for the relevant key words, you can isolate a (probably large) set of web pages that may have something useful to say about it. Some of these pages will have a large number of incoming links. These are obviously popular, but are they authoritative? To answer that question, you need to judge the quality of the pages that point to them.

Here is where the notion of "hub" pages comes in. A hub has a large number of outgoing links to pages on a common topic. It can be thought of as a recommender of information sources on the topic. An authoritative page is one that is recommended by a sufficient number of good hubs. A good hub is one that recommends a sufficient number of authoritative destination pages.

If this sounds a bit circular, don't worry. There are at least two methods by which such recursive problems can be solved. The first way is a bit mathematical, involving Eigenvectors and matrix algebra. The good news is that you don't need to dip into that topic because the internet has so many hundreds of millions of pages that doing a matrix inversion to find these Eigenvectors is a practical impossibility.

The second way is to put ratings on all the web sites (perhaps a rating of one for every site initially), and then modify the ratings according to some rule about the ratings of the sites that point to it (for authorities) and the ratings of the sites it points to (for hubs). This calculation needs to be done in a series of waves or iterations. Kleinberg showed that the number of iterations you need to find a stable set of ratings, while not exactly small, was manageable for a modern computer.

Using this procedure, Kleinberg was able to find the top several authorities on each of many topics, ranging from java, to censorship, to search engines, to Bill Gates. This approach was remarkably successful in eliminating the spam and getting to the point. If you have used Google, which employs a similar type of approach, you will know how successfully the topology of the web can be used to find authoritative sources. In my humble opinion, this is one of the triumphs of our age.

Can this type of approach help us to find news we can trust?

Human links

Are there human equivalents to hubs and authorities? Can this topological analysis of the internet be applied to that subtle web of connections between real actual people? I think so.

Journalist Malcolm Gladwell touched on this topic in an enormously influential book about how social movements happen. He observed that one reason for the fame of Paul Revere is that he was well connected to a lot of people in the colony of Massachusetts. Revere, who is best remembered for his midnight ride to alert the colony of an imminent attack by the British Army, was not the only midnight rider that night. Another one, William Dawes, had a similar mission in a different part of the colony. While Revere managed to summon a sizeable militia to respond to the attack, Dawes was singularly unsuccessful in rousing the fighters on his route. The minutemen responded to Paul Revere because of who he was. In Gladwell's words, he was a 'connector' and Dawes was not. For our purposes, we could think of him as a human equivalent to a hub on the internet. People went where Revere pointed.

Gladwell's book, *The Tipping Point*, also featured another type of person whom he called a 'maven.' A maven is an expert in a particular field. Mavens have some interesting personal traits, and Gladwell describes them at length. For our purposes, though, what is important is how to find them, because mavens are the human equivalents of the authorities that we are so desperately searching for.

Mavens and connectors have a symbiotic, mutually reinforcing relationship. A maven gains in stature and relevance by being connected to those people who value her knowledge, and a good connector can do that. Similarly, a connector gains credibility by having valuable content to communicate to his network. A good maven can provide that content.

In a practical sense, the way to find a maven is to ask a connector. Finding a connector is not so hard, because he tends to be the sort of person that seems to know everybody.

Finding a good connector, and thereby a good maven is a little more difficult, and for that some version of Kleinberg's iterative algorithm is probably necessary. Is that something we can do?

Is it practical for a normal person to do this?

I struggle to make sense of the Electronic Program Guide on television. Many others struggle to understand the full range of news sources that are available when they want to receive news. How is a normal person ever going to do what Jon Kleinberg did, given the mighty calculations he needed to do to accomplish it? In short, won't the daunting iterative calculation of hubs and authorities be a stumbling block for the person in the street to evaluate sources of news?

It doesn't need to be. First of all, the evaluation doesn't need to be done every day. A reputable source yesterday will probably still be reputable today. Quality changes will take time—both improvements and deteriorations.

Second of all, people constantly underestimate the amount of computing power that is available to them. If you have a laptop computer that was built post-2015 it could probably do all the calculations that were needed to land a man on the moon in 1969. It's quite possible that your telephone could, too. A lack of computing power is one problem that none of us in the first world have to worry about.

What have we been misunderstanding about the future? As far as politicians are concerned, we have been far too accepting of their feeble claims that they should draw district boundaries, that political parties are good for democracy and that political donations (aka bribes) are necessary for them to function. We need to apply the same discipline to them that they apply to welfare recipients.

Threats and conspiracies are two issues that we have completely misunderstood. We could probably go much further than we have with threat elimination, but some level of coexistence with threats is politically expedient.

Conspiracies are an endangered species, if only we could recognise them as such. I don't suggest that we try to preserve them through a hunting ban or captive breeding program. I do say that we should not waste much time worrying about something that is so unlikely to bite us.

On a positive note, we have underestimated the upside of the internet and internet searching tools. If I am right, there is enormous potential to improve the quality of the news we receive by following the methods of Kleinberg, Brin and Page. We have been far too accepting of outright lying by people in power, and these methods may give us a way to do something about that problem.

8
WHAT NEXT?

Things have become very confusing in the modern world. I've tried to explain why that happened. The cost of broadcasting messages to a wide audience has dropped to nearly zero, so everyone's doing it. Developing a consensus view about anything has become difficult, in part because there is nothing and no one to force you to confront facts that conflict with your worldview. No common basis in fact means no common understanding.

Science is losing its centuries-old war with what I will call "religion", although many will not recognise it as such. I don't know what else you could call the worship of autocrats. We've turned back the clock on the separation of Church and State. Various belief systems are invading the policy space that should be governed instead by facts and logical reasoning.

Instead of being right, in this fractured landscape, those who want to be noticed focus on "cutting through" the noise. They've worked out that the way to do that is to be entertaining. So they entertain a lot of loony ideas without regard to the consequences. The attitude of these leaders to the climate, infectious disease control, and an orderly society is cavalier.

There is a general assumption that the planet's stabilising feedback loops can handle anything that people throw at it, so why not have fun? Most likely, that assumption is wrong. Every day, our planet comes to resemble Mars a little more. Mars used to have oceans of water before their own episode of catastrophic climate change.

People are comforted by the ingenuity of the human race, and assume we'll find a way through. Science will save the day. Oh wait. We don't believe what scientists say any more.

8.1 What if our problems suddenly went away?

There is one scenario that gives me some cheer. Let us imagine that we prepare modern-day versions of Noah's ark to help us transition to a new planetary home. Trump and his followers take the first ark and blast off to their manifest destiny among the stars. After that ship launches, the rest of us re-evaluate our situation and find that we can make our existing planet work very well after all, so we stay and enact sensible laws and thereby solve our most pressing current problems. Call me a hopeless optimist, but that way everyone would get what they wanted.

Of course, a moment's reflection will reveal the inadequacies of that solution. From the standpoint of those on the B-ark, there would be social problems in the immediate aftermath of blast-off. The lack of any out-group to demonise would temporarily stall efforts to organise government or mobilise the base to vote. I assume that problem would be solvable by finding some new personal characteristic by which to identify and repress a new minority.

Their next problem, finding somewhere to land, would take some solving, particularly as they left all the qualified scientists behind. The list of potentially habitable exoplanets within 100 light years of Earth is short. A full evaluation of a candidate planet may require going there to check it out. As the B-ark would not travel at (or anywhere near) the speed of light, actually getting to a new home would realistically take more than one lifetime. Patience is bound to wear thin.

But if we assume all these problems will be solved, one remains. There is a reasonable chance that the new planet, which is perfectly suitable for hosting carbon-based life forms, will be occupied when the B-arkers arrive. Things could go one of two ways. Either the interstellar travellers successfully colonise the new world despite the indigenous inhabitants, or the indigenous inhabitants eat them for breakfast. Without knowing more, it is probably a 50-50 bet.

One can easily foresee these stumbling blocks: disharmony among the travellers, the possibility of not finding any habitable planet, and the risk of losing a war of conquest with the resident aliens. Any one of these inconvenient truths should give the B-arkers pause. Of course, if they were the sort of people to be bothered by inconvenient truth they probably would not have boarded the ship in the first place.

Still, it is reasonably foreseeable that the B-arkers would decide to return to Earth before too long. How welcome would they be?

8.2 Those of us left behind

Meanwhile back on Earth, it is also foreseeable that the social dynamics that gave rise to figures like Trump, Bolsonaro, or Putin would generate a new one to fill any vacuum. The replacement might not have quite the same talent for generating outrage, but hopefuls would undoubtedly chance their arm and some will be successful. Chaos is a determined adversary. The second law of thermodynamics is difficult to understand, but no one really doubts that entropy is on the rise.

Many people will happily tell you what you should do. Book authors are high on that list. In my case, I will just offer this. Rather than wishing our problems away, perhaps we should come to terms with what has gone wrong with our understanding of the world. Misunderstanding causes dysfunction. We do things that make us worse off, thinking they will help us. We fail to do things we need to because we think they will harm us or because it never occurred to us. It is like trying to drive a car in a fog. When the fog lifts and you can see what you're facing, you will know what to do.

Notes

Chapter 2.2.1 – Three worlds
Karl Marx. *Das Kapital*. London (1867).

Chapter 2.3.4 – Disinformation
Robert Putnam. *Bowling Alone*. Simon & Schuster, New York (2000).

Chapter 3.1 – The dismal side of the force
Thomas Malthus. *An Essay on the Principle of Population* (1798).

Chapter 3.1.1 – The dismal science
John Maynard Keynes. "In the long run we are all dead."
A Tract on Monetary Reform (1923), Ch. 3, p. 80.

Chapter 3.1.2 – Modern limits to growth
The Club of Rome. *Limits to Growth*. Earth Island Limited,
London (1972).

Chapter 3.1.3 – It works in theory, but does it work in fact?
Peter Turchin and Sergey Nefedov. *Secular Cycles*.
Princeton University Press, New Jersey (2009).

Chapter 3.1.5 – What economists say about this
Becker, Murphy and Tamura. "Human Capital, Fertility,
and Economic Growth." Journal of Political Economy, 1990, vol 98,
no 5, part 2.

Chapter 3.2.5 – Motivation and personality
Abraham Maslow. *Motivation and Personality*. Harper & Row,
New York (1954).

Chapter 3.2.7 – Real per capita growth is stalling
ENGEL CURVES Entry for The New Palgrave Dictionary of
Economics, 2nd edition Arthur Lewbel. (revised Sept., 2006)
https://www2.bc.edu/arthur-lewbel/palengel.pdf

Robert Gordon. "Is U.S. Economic Growth Over? Faltering Innovation
Confronts the Six Headwinds." NBER Working Paper No. 18315
(August 2012). http://www.nber.org/papers/w18315

Chapter 6 – Gerrymander
Washington Post maps on gerrymandering:
https://www.washingtonpost.com/news/wonk/wp/2014/06/03/
this-computer-programmer-solved-gerrymandering-in-his-spare-
time/?utm_term=.acdd90c20786
https://www.washingtonpost.com/news/wonk/wp/2016/01/13/
this-is-actually-what-america-would-look-like-without-
gerrymandering/?utm_term=.ed9e47c13a02

Chapter 7.3.1 – Science citations
    Sergey Brin and Lawrence Page. "The Anatomy of a Large-Scale Hypertextual Web Search Engine." (1998) http://ilpubs.stanford. edu:8090/361/

Chapter 7.3.3 – Before the Page Rank algorithm
    Jon Kleinberg. "Authoritative Sources in a Hyperlinked Environment." (1998) https://www.cs.cornell.edu/home/kleinber/auth.pdf

Chapter 7.3.4 – Human links
    Malcolm Gladwell. *The Tipping Point*. Abacus. Little Brown, London (2001).

Endnotes

1   Becker, Murphy and Tamura, "Human Capital, Fertility, and Economic Growth", *Journal of Political Economy,* 1990, vol 98, no 5, part 2.

2   In fact, even though it has been softened to a two child limit since 2015, the birth rate has not increased markedly. China is presently facing a demographic problem in that the ratio of older retired people to younger working people who must support them is rapidly increasing.

3   I wrote this before the Capitol insurrection of 6 January 2021, which was a living example of a group of unhappy armed voters trying to overthrow the US government. The failure of these mutineers supports my conclusion. I recognise, though, that the fact they came so close to achieving some of their immediate tactical objectives must give us all pause to reflect.

4   This was written when Donald Trump was the President.

5   Thalidomide hero found guilty of scientific fraud – *The New Scientist*, 27 February 1991

6   *"FTC Policy Statement on Deception"* (PDF). October 14, 1983. p. 4.

7   Rather than catalogue this mountainous evidence, I will simply note that it would be illogical for political parties to spend the astronomical sums that they do if propaganda didn't work. Are political advertisements lies? Let's put it this way: when candidate C and candidate T are making diametrically opposite claims, they can't both be right.

8   https://www.theguardian.com/world/2015/sep/01/australian-and-thai-journalists-found-not-guilty-of-defaming-thai-navy

9   https://www.reuters.com/article/egypt-politics/egypts-sisi-says-defaming-army-or-police-is-treason-idUSL4N1QJ4A6

10   *"Natural Resource Diversity and Democracy,"* Mike Smart, Economic Papers, Volume 28, No. 4, December 2009, 366-375.

11   Space does not permit me to do justice to Godel's work here. However, an excellent explanation for the non-mathematician is available in Douglas Hofstadter's 1980 masterpiece "Godel, Escher Bach: an eternal golden braid." It is a long book, but full of diagrams, word puzzles and other thought-provoking stuff (including translations of Lewis Carroll's poem Jabberwocky into French and German). Hofstadter is a professor of computer science.

12   That is no coincidence. The Page-rank algorithm had its origins in the meta-analysis of scientific citations.

13   https://imprimis.hillsdale.edu/emfree-to-chooseem-a-conversation-with-milton-friedman/

[14] For example, Ireland until recently, India v Pakistan, partitions imposed on Middle Eastern nations by the British, the former Yugoslavia, Israel v Palestine, etc.

[15] The issue of voter fraud has received a lot of attention in the aftermath of the 2020 American presidential election. Despite the sound and fury, no credible evidence has been produced of a result-altering fraud.

[16] Brin, S and Page, L, "The Anatomy of a Large-Scale Hypertextual Web Search Engine." (1998) http://ilpubs.stanford.edu:8090/361/

www.ingramcontent.com/pod-product-compliance
Lightning Source LLC
LaVergne TN
LVHW052032080426
835513LV00018B/2289